THIRD EYE AWAKENING

3 BOOKS IN 1

DISCOVER THE BENEFITS OF OPENING YOUR THIRD EYE WITH CHAKRAS AND REIKI HEALING AND INCREASE YOUR SELF-AWARENESS THROUGH GUIDED MEDITATIONS

Caroline Kirkman

© **Copyright 2020 - All rights reserved.**

The content contained within this book may not be reproduced, duplicated or transmitted without direct written permission from the author or the publisher.

Under no circumstances will any blame or legal responsibility be held against the publisher, or author, for any damages, reparation, or monetary loss due to the information contained within this book. Either directly or indirectly.

Legal Notice:

This book is copyright protected. This book is only for personal use. You cannot amend, distribute, sell, use, quote or paraphrase any part, or the content within this book, without the consent of the author or publisher.

Disclaimer Notice:

Please note the information contained within this document is for educational and entertainment purposes only. All effort has been executed to present accurate, up to date, and reliable, complete information. No warranties of any kind are declared or implied. Readers acknowledge that the author is not engaging in the rendering of legal, financial, medical or professional advice. The content within this book has been derived from various sources. Please consult a licensed professional before attempting any techniques outlined in this book.

By reading this document, the reader agrees that under no circumstances is the author responsible for any losses, direct or indirect, which are incurred as a result of the use of information contained within this document, including, but not limited to, — errors, omissions, or inaccuracies.

TABLE OF CONTENTS

BOOK 1) CHAKRAS FOR BEGINNERS

INTRODUCTION 13
    THE HISTORY OF THE CHAKRAS 19
CHAPTER 1: CROWN CHAKRA 23
    FOODS AND DRINKS 24
    ASSOCIATED CRYSTALS 25
    MEDITATION POSES 28
CHAPTER 2: THE THIRD EYE 31
    SIGNS AND SYMPTOMS OF AWAKENING THE THIRD EYE 39
    FOODS AND DRINKS 43
    ASSOCIATED CRYSTALS 43
    MEDITATION POSES 46
CHAPTER 3: THROAT CHAKRA 49
    EXERCISES 59
    FOODS AND DRINKS 59
    HEALING THROAT CHAKRA 59
    ASSOCIATED CRYSTALS 62
    MEDITATION POSES 65
CHAPTER 4: HEART CHAKRA 69
    EXERCISES 72
    FOODS AND DRINKS 72
    ASSOCIATED CRYSTALS 73
    MEDITATION POSES 76
CHAPTER 5: SOLAR PLEXUS CHAKRA 79
    EXERCISES 80
    FOODS AND DRINKS 81
    ASSOCIATED CRYSTALS 81

MEDITATION POSES	84
CHAPTER 6: SACRAL CHAKRA	87
EXERCISES FOR SACRAL CHAKRA	89
FOODS AND DRINKS FOR SACRAL CHAKRA	89
ASSOCIATED CRYSTALS	90
MEDITATION POSE	92
CHAPTER 7: BASE/ROOT CHAKRA	95
EXERCISES FOR ROOT CHAKRA	104
FOODS AND DRINKS FOR ROOT CHAKRA	105
ASSOCIATED CRYSTALS	106
MEDITATION POSE	110
CONCLUSION	111
REFERENCES	113

BOOK 2) REIKI FOR BEGINNERS

INTRODUCTION	119
CHAPTER ONE: THE REIKI STORY	123
CHAPTER TWO: HOW TO LEARN REIKI	131
STEPS FOR LEARNING REIKI	132
STEP 1: CONNECT WITH THE UNIVERSAL ENERGY	132
STEP 2: PERFORM AN AURA SCAN	134
STEP 3: REALIZE YOUR HEALING INTENTION	135
STEP 4: ACTIVATE REIKI SYMBOLS	136
STEP 5: GUIDE HEALING ENERGY	138
STEP 6: CLOSE YOUR CONNECTION	139
STEP 7: EXPAND YOUR ENERGY CHANNELS	139
CHAPTER THREE: HOW A REIKI SESSION WORKS	143
THE TRADITIONAL POSITIONS OF THE HANDS	147
HOW REIKI SELF-TREATMENT WORKS	150
ORGANIZE YOUR PRACTICE	151
HOW DISTANT REIKI TREATMENT WORKS	152
FOUR FIELDS OF ENERGY	152

How to Do Distance Healing 153
Chapter Four: Ailments Healed With Reiki 159
Different Illnesses Reiki Treatment Can Cure 160
Headache and Backache 160
Backache 161
Kidney and Liver Problems 162
Liver Complaints 163

Arthritis, Pain, and Fractures 163
Arthritis 163
Pain 163
Fractures 164

Diabetes, Asthma, and Heart Attack 165
Diabetes 165
Asthma 165
Heart Attack 166

Epileptic Fits and Weight Problem 167
Epileptic Fits 167
Weight Problem 167
Anemia 168
Cancer and Fever 169
For Frail Recipients 169
Tongue Cancer 170
Leukemia 170
Fever 171

Cramps and Leg Problems 172
Cramps 172
Leg Problems 173

Blood Pressure and Bleeding 173
Bleeding 174
High Blood Pressure 174
Low Blood Pressure 175
Detoxification 175

Bladder Problems and Acne 177
Bladder Problems 177
Acne 178
Rheumatism 178

Menstrual Complaints and Childbirth 179
Childbirth 180

NOSE COMPLAINTS.. 180
   NOSE BLOCKAGE.. 181
   SINUS PROBLEM 181
   NOSEBLEED 182

COLD, COUGH, INSOMNIA, AND ALLERGIES.......................... 183
   COLD 183
   INSOMNIA.. 183
   ALLERGIES... 184

CHAPTER FIVE: ADDITIONAL BENEFITS OF REIKI 187

ADDITIONAL PSYCHOLOGICAL AND MENTAL BENEFITS OF REIKI
.... 187
   ACCELERATES SELF-HEALING ABILITY 188
   GETS RID OF BAD KARMA 188
   IMPROVES QUALITY OF LIFE... 189
   IMPROVES SLEEP 190
   PROMOTES SPIRITUAL GROWTH AND EMOTIONAL CLEANSING
   191
   SPEEDS UP RECOVERY FROM ILLNESSES AND SURGERIES
   192
   GUARANTEES MENTAL FREEDOM 193
   ASSISTS THE BODY IN ELIMINATING TOXINS 194
   PROMOTES NATURAL BALANCE BETWEEN MIND, BODY, AND
   SPIRIT 195
   REDUCES DEPRESSION AND ANXIETY 196
   EASES PAIN 197
   REDUCES STRESS.. 198
   HEALS INFECTION AND INFLAMMATION............................. 199
   HELPS YOU FEEL EMPOWERED 200
   INCREASES CREATIVE JUICES... 201
   HELPS YOU MAGNETIZE ABUNDANCE 202

CHAPTER SIX: THE CONCEPT OF CONTINUITY WITH REIKI...... 204

HOW TO SUSTAIN REIKI IN YOUR LIFE..................................... 205
   SHOW UP FOR SESSIONS... 205
   BE ATTENTIVE TO YOUR BODY 206
   LEARN MORE.. 208
   DON'T BE SELFISH 209
   SPREAD THE WORD, HELP OTHERS 210
   EXPERIENCE AND HEART (PASSION).................................... 212
   WORK WITH AN ILLUMINED BEING..................................... 215

HOW TO GET HELP FROM AN ILLUMINED BEING................... 215

CONCLUSION 220
REFERENCES 222

BOOK 3) GUIDED MINDFULNESS MEDITATION

INTRODUCTION 227
CHAPTER 1: WHAT IS MINDFULNESS? 229
    MINDFULNESS AND ITS IMPORTANCE IN BRINGING DOWN STRESS, ANXIETY, AND PANIC ATTACKS 229
    WHAT MAKES IT DIFFERENT? 231
    MINDFULNESS AND THE CONCEPT OF AWARENESS 232
    IT WASN'T MEANT TO BE LIKE THIS 233
    WHAT CLUTTERS THE MIND 235
    ADVANTAGES OF BEING MINDFUL 236
    MINDFULNESS AND MINDFULNESS MEDITATION 238
CHAPTER 2: YOUR WAY INTO MINDFULNESS MEDITATION 241
    IMPORTANCE OF IDEAL SETTINGS FOR MEDITATION 241
    THE ESSENTIALS 242
        PLACE 242
        TIME 245
        DURATION 247
        CLOTHING 248
    THE POSTURE 248
        IMPORTANT TIPS 249
        COMMON MEDITATION POSTURES 252
    LEARNING TO FOCUS INWARDS 259
        STEADINESS OF BODY 259
        RHYTHMIC BREATHING 260
        RELAXATION 261
    FINDING THE MOTIVATION 262
    MINDFULNESS MEDITATION TECHNIQUES 263
CHAPTER 3: LEARNING TO BECOME MORE MINDFUL 269
CHAPTER 4: IMPORTANT BREATHING EXERCISES 277

- CHAPTER 5: PRACTICING THE ART OF MINDFUL BREATHING . 283
  - MINDFUL BREATHING MEDITATION 283
- CHAPTER 6: INITIATION 293
  - BODY SCAN MEDITATION 293
    - THROUGH THIS MEDITATION: 294
    - PREPARATION 294
    - MEDITATION 294
  - BREATHING SPACE MEDITATION 302
- CHAPTER 7: RELAXATION 311
  - BODY SCAN MEDITATION 311
  - MINDFULNESS MEDITATION FOR LIVING IN THE PRESENT ... 322
  - MINDFULNESS MEDITATION FOR REDUCING ANXIETY AND STRESS 334
  - LOVING-KINDNESS MEDITATION 347
- CHAPTER 8: PRACTICE SHORT 3 MINUTE GUIDED MEDITATION FOR BRINGING PEACE TO MIND 363
  - 5 MINUTE GUIDED MEDITATION FOR BUILDING FOCUS 367
  - 7 MINUTE GUIDED MEDITATION FOR BREATH CONTROL AND RELAXATION 372
- CONCLUSION 380

Chakras for Beginners

Healing Yourself With Chakras and Meditation. A Complete Guide to Third Eye and Chakra Healing for Starters With Practical Exercises to Balance Your Chakras

Caroline Kirkman

Introduction

Do you feel that you are having trouble communicating with others? Do you feel that your thoughts are always in a jumble? Do you have issues with feeling bouts of anger and humiliation on a daily basis? If you are experiencing any of these issues in your life, you may be dealing with an issue of a chakra or more out of line.

Our current lifestyles are often not conducive to helping us to live a happy and fulfilled life. We eat foods that are not that healthy for us, we participate in activities that are not the best for us and can make us sick, we have bad thoughts and actions, and we just don't take as much time to take care of ourselves. All of this is going to come together to make it more likely that our life energy is going to be used up in the wrong way, and our whole bodies are going to suffer.

I am sure you have already heard the word "chakra" before, but do you really know what it means? Chakra is a Sanskrit word that denotes the word "wheel." Chakras are life-giving wheels located all throughout the body—specifically in 7 parts of the body. These life-giving wheels are believed to be where energy is stored. The stored energy is known as "prana" or "chi." So, essentially, chakras are energetic power centers that take in and distribute energy all through the body. The seven major chakras in the physical body match up with the endocrine glands and nerve plexus.

Chakras are considered to be responsible for the flow of energy all through the body of an organism. And this is where the Eastern philosophy places an emphasis on "blocked chakra wheels" which can prevent the energy from flowing through the body leading to various pains, diseases, and illnesses.

Further, chakras are considered to be completely linked to one another—just like all the cells, tissues, and organs of your body are. If the energy flows through the chakras smoothly and freely, then your body is healthy. Thus, blockage of the chakras can affect not only the physical body but also can affect us emotionally and mentally.

For the most part, we are uncertain about the best way to take care of ourselves. We may try to eat a diet that is a bit healthier or we may work on getting some exercise. But unless we are able to work on those chakras and get them all lined up and working in tune together, we are always going to suffer and not feel as good as we should.

You will see that each of the chakras has a name, and this is significant because we will be detailing how to free up that chakra and will be calling it by its official name. For the time being, look at the throat chakra because this is one that people in the Western world understand. When you have pain in the neck, chances are that stress is causing it. There seems to be a blockage and this is where stress usually hits. Just as this chakra rules the health of the throat area, the others have a specific area that they cover. The idea is that energy should be able to run freely between all of the chakras and when there is a blockage of any one of the chakras, this stops the energy system from functioning as it should. Let us start at the top of the head and explain what each of these chakras does because it's vital that you understand their purpose.

Each of the chakras are important to the body. They are going to help you to feel whole, and even healthier. When one of the chakras is not working the way that it should, there can be issues in the body. For example, if you have chronic headaches, it could be because your third eye chakra needs some attention. Each of these are portals to the universe and if you don't take care of them the proper way, something in your body or your life is going to suffer.

Each of your chakras is going to have an important job to do to help you out. First, it is up to you to help keep them open and working properly. They need to be able to reach out to the universe is the right manner, allowing enough of the energy to come into the body to help you connect to the universe but not enough so that you are going to be overwhelmed; learning the right balance between these is going to take a bit of time.

Plus, once you have made sure that these chakras are going to reach the universe the right way you need to also make sure that they are able to interact with each other. There needs to be a clear path so that the energy between the chakras is able to flow freely between each other.

When the chakras are not open to each other and they aren't letting the right amount of energy come in through the universe (either too much energy or too little), that is when you are going to start seeing some issues in your life. You may experience issues with headaches, you could have some trouble with your relationships. It is important to learn how to take care of these chakras so that they work well together and with the universe and so that you don't end up with as much trouble with your life energy as before.

The chakras are our centers of energy, located right along the midline of the body. There are seven major ones, although some schools of thought about the chakras will include a few more of them as well. These chakras are going to all work together and when they are in great working order and receiving the energy that they need, you will find that your body feels great, you can be true to yourself and to others, and you will show the right amount of love that you need. Your life is basically going to be balanced as well without any of the common ailments that most people complain about.

On the other hand, you need to spend some time working on your chakras if something isn't working out the way that you want. If you feel that you are dealing with bouts of anger and jealousy all the time, if you have pain around the body, or your focus is all out of order, it implies that one or more of your chakras are not working the way that they should.

These chakras can also work together. If you find that one is not working right, is not open the way that it should be, and you don't fix it right away, you will eventually have the rest of the chakras go out of line as well. You need to focus on the chakra or two that are bothering you, and then the rest of them can start to align themselves properly as well.

Each of the chakras is going to have different levels of activity. When the chakras are open and allowing the energy to come through, the chakras are considered to be operating in their normal fashion.

Ideally, all of the chakras will contribute to our being. We all have instincts and if they are working properly, they will help to influence our thinking and our feelings. However, this is not usually the case because the chakras, and our intuition, will not be working correctly. Some of the chakras may not be opened up like they should. When one or two chakras are down, all the other ones are going to become overactive and this can cause us many issues as well.

In the ideal state, all of the chakras will work together and be balanced. But with our modern lives, we are going to find it is harder to live a life where the chakras are in good working order. We are always on the run, trying to get things all done and barely being able to take care of ourselves. But if you want to really enjoy a good life that is happy and healthy, you need to take a step back, and learn how to take care of these chakras.

Luckily, once you realize which of the chakras is out of line and needs to be balanced, there are quite a few techniques you will be able to use in order to balance out the chakras. Mostly, the techniques are going to help you to open up the chakras that are needed, because this will often fix up the issues with the other ones being overactive most of the time.

To better visualize a chakra, it is likened to a spinning ball in the form of a lotus that moves up and down the spine as it spins continuously. It is in a constant spin to renew, rejuvenate and move energy all through the body. It moves smoothly and speedily without stopping. Chakras also feature a special color of the aura it creates and this color can also change accordingly. If a person is angry or ill, the movement of the chakra is affected—this can mean it is moving through the body in a disoriented manner or spinning too fast or too slow. The chakra colors can also change, dissolve completely or fade when an individual is physically or emotionally impaired. You will learn more about this in the subsequent chapters. And further, the chakras cannot be physically seen in our body because they exist only as psychic centers.

Ever felt pain and pressure in the back of your neck? The chances are that you are stressed and that the chakra located in the neck region is taking on all of that negative energy. Negative energy stops you in your tracks and can really make life difficult. This chakra is probably one of the most obvious in the body even to those who know little about the chakra system. However, do you know where the other chakras are located? In this chapter, we make you aware of them so that you know from your own experiences which chakra is giving you problems.

The crown chakra is situated at the head's top. The third eye chakra is located between the lines of your eyebrows. The throat chakra placement is obvious. The heart chakra can be found located in the center of your body at heart level. The sacral chakra is just below your navel, while your solar plexus chakra is about 3 inches above the belly button. The base chakra is located at the base of the spine.

You can see that these are represented by colors and symbols, each of which have meaning. However, as a beginner, it's more important that you know which problems relate to each of the chakras, so that you can perform the exercises or activities needed to open up that chakra in times of need. Let's run through the kinds of things that each of these chakras is responsible for, so that you gain a better understanding of them. It is not as complex as acupuncture because in acupuncture, there are many pressure points. Thus learning about the chakras is much easier for the beginner than learning other systems of energy control.

The Crown Chakra – If the crown chakra is out of whack, you may be experiencing depression. You may also have problems with your concentration. Any mental blockage of any kind can come from this region. In fact, if you are short tempered because of sounds or the density of light, perhaps it is this chakra that is out of alignment. In a later chapter, we will talk about balancing the chakra responsible for your lack of alignment, though for now, we merely discuss the illnesses likely to be caused by a blockage in a certain chakra.

The Third Eye Chakra – This is responsible for all kinds of things, including blurred vision, lack of intuitive thought, hearing loss, sinus problems etc., but it doesn't stop there. If you have emotional problems then this chakra is like to play a part. If you feel the need to exaggerate to gain the attention of others, then this is a weakness that could be accounted for by the blockage of this chakra.

The Throat Chakra – As we already explained, stress can cause this chakra to be blocked, but there are other health issues as well. For example, thyroid conditions, facial pain or even ear infections can all be caused by the blockage of this particular chakra.

The Heart Chakra – This is an important chakra when it comes to illnesses that are serious. Lung disease, heart problems and pains in the lower arm can all be attributable to a blockage of this chakra. If you find that your upper back area has problems or your shoulders hurt, this is also likely to be the chakra that is causing that pain. Emotional imbalances may be the cause of this chakra being out of alignment too, and this includes feelings of jealousy, insecurity with relationships or any anger that comes from your relationships with others.

The Solar Plexus Chakra – This chakra is related to digestive problems, gall bladder problems and even chronic fatigue. That feeling of butterflies in the stomach or nervousness when faced by new things comes from this region, as well as fears of being rejected.

The Sacral Chakra – If you suffer from urinary problems, this is likely to be the offender. Pains that arise in the lower back area can also come from this chakra, as can liver problems.

This chakra is a great chakra to balance because it gives you dynamism and confidence.

The Root Chakra – This accounts for problems below the area where the chakra is located and that can include knee problems, immunity problems, prostate gland problems, sciatica and even illnesses such as constipation or ailments caused by eating disorders. The root chakra also acts as the main chakra to take account of people's feelings of having all of their needs in life fulfilled, such as housing or being able to support oneself. This chakra is likely to be blocked when your living situation feels out of control.

As you can see, we have generalized each of the areas of the chakras so that you get a clue as to which chakra is blocked, depending upon the difficulty that you are currently encountering.

The History of the Chakras

While the chakras are part of an ancient tradition, they are starting to make a reappearance in modern times. There are many new interpretations of their meaning and their functions, and sometimes it is easy to get confused since there are so many ways to think about these chakras. While the popularity is starting to make the chakras more of a word that people recognize, there are a lot of times when this information is going to be erroneous, conflicting, and even confusing. Before you work on making the chakras a part of your life, it is important to understand some of the history that comes with these chakras which can better explain how they should be used.

The Vedas are some of the oldest written traditions from the area of South Asia, and they were recorded from the oral tradition of the upper caste Brahmins (Judith, n.d.). The original meaning of this word chakra is "wheel" which refers to the chariot wheels that were used by the rulers of that time

("Brief history of chakras", n.d.). The word has also been used in these texts as a metaphor for the sun, which is able to traverse the world just like a triumphant chariot and will denote the eternal wheel of time, which also represents balance and order, just like the idea of the wheel and what the chakras are going to focus on.

The birth of the chakras was said to herald in a brand new age, and they were often described as being preceded by a disk of light, such as the halo of Christ, but there was a spinning disk that was in front of them. It is also said that Vishnu, the Hindu god of preservation, descended to Earth, carrying the chakra, a club, a conch shell, and a lotus flower.

In these texts, there are also some mentions of the chakras being like a psychic center of consciousness in several different versions of this text including the Yoga Sutras of Patanjali and the Yoga Upanishads. The implied goal of yoga was to rise above nature and the world that you are living in, in order to find the realization of a pure consciousness, one that was free from any fluctuations that came in with the emotions and the mind. Yet the word yoga stands for yoke or union, so the realization that happens in between consciousness and realization must ultimately reintegrate with nature to get a higher synthesis.

So, since the idea of yoga and the chakras arose inside of the same tradition, the tantric tradition, it is no wonder that they are often associated with each other. As we will discuss later on, you will find that yoga is one of the ways that you will be able to bring the chakras into line because they were both developed in the same tradition and both can be used at the same time.

In the traditional ideation of the chakras, there are seven basic ones and they are all going to exist inside of your body. Through modern physiology, it is easy to see that the seven chakras are going to correspond exactly to the main nerve ganglia inside of the body, which all come from the spinal column. While many people assume that these chakras have nothing to do with them any longer, the chakras were well placed, put into specific parts of the body where nerves are located and where different parts can influence how the rest of the body is going to react. It is interesting that the chakras were able to develop based on these thoughts, even before all of the nerves and pressure points would have been realized by modern science.

In addition to the main seven chakras that most people concentrate on, there are a few minor chakras that are mentioned inside of the ancient texts. For example, there is the soma chakra which you will be able to find right above the third eye chakra and then there is the ananda kanda lotus, which is going to be near the heart chakra, plus a few more based on how deeply into the ancient texts you choose to dive.

Many people assume that the chakras are an ancient idea that you shouldn't pay any attention to in the modern day. They figure that the chakras have nothing to do with how they live their present-day lives and they may assume it was all a bunch of spirituality that is purely fictitious. But in reality, you will find that in modern times, the chakras are more important than ever. We need to understand how easily we can get out of balance. We are always running around, always stressed out and worried, and we often have trouble with our relationships. Chakras are able to get these back into balance and restore harmony in our bodies and our lives.

People who practice balancing their chakras are going to be so much healthier and happier, and better able to get through the day, compared to others who don't even believe in the chakras and just keep slogging through all of the negativity in their lives. It is definitely worth your time to ensure that you are able to get the great life that you would like without all the issues.

Chapter 1: Crown Chakra

Once all of the other needs have been met, the human psyche thirsts for awareness, knowledge, and unity. The endeavors of seeking knowledge differ in the topic for each individual depending on their interests and personality; some study spirituality intently, others take a more academic or practical approach, but the principles remain the same. The need for a sense of unity is one of the most powerful needs we experience as humans. There comes a sense of enlightenment once we realize that everything is connected in an intricate, elaborate tapestry, where every single thread plays an important part and, in its existence, contributes to all of the other threads.

At the top of the chakra order and the crown of the head lies the crown or sahasrara chakra (Olesen, 2014). This chakra connects us to the universe and spiritual divinity. This chakra relies on the idea that everything in the universe is connected, that we are all one and united. An open crown chakra is one of enlightenment, awareness, and freedom from most negatively judgmental tendencies. An underactive crown results in a stubborn, unadaptable way of thinking, an insistence that your ideas are right no matter what evidence is presented against you, and a refusal to acknowledge perspectives other than your own. An overactive crown chakra entails you are overthinking things, obsessing so much on a matter of the mind or spirituality that you are ignoring your other needs, your bodily health, or your outside life.

The crown chakra can become offset when there is excessive attachment present in a person's life. This attachment can be forged to a place, materialistic objects, an idea or belief system, or a person. The person becomes increasingly dependent on the subject of their attachment and cannot fathom life without the subject. They're generally unable to see the situation in a rational way and are looking through a sort of tunnel vision. This imbalance violates the person's sense of a right to know, and they do not feel they should acknowledge anything outside of their narrow viewpoint.

A closed or unbalanced crown chakra can be connected to sensitivity to light and sound, neurological disorders, arrogance, entitlement, restlessness, boredom, sleep disorders, mental illnesses, learning disabilities, and even comas.

As with the third eye chakra before it, the crown chakra is fed by periods of silence. Turning off background noise whenever possible and clearing your mind is essential to opening the crown chakra. Luckily, by the time you've reached this final chakra in the system, you probably have had plenty of practice in clearing your thoughts, grounding, and achieving a peaceful state.

All of the things you've done to support and open the other chakras can be applied to the final crown chakra. Connecting with nature, keeping a journal, paying attention to your body and self, meditation, essential oils and incense, chanting mantras and positive affirmations such as "I am divine" or "Ohm," and creative activities used to balance the previous chakras can all be used for the benefit of the crown chakra.

This is the most general chakra of the seven in that it doesn't correspond to particular dietary needs or particularly specific practices. Thoughtfulness and light are the primary elements of this chakra, and so engaging in logical activities and focusing especially on thoughtfulness and learning are helpful. This might include doing puzzles, playing logic-based or strategy games, reading, and studying different materials. Immersing yourself in plenty of gentle natural lighting can also contribute to healing the crown chakra. Consider adjusting the lighting in your home and workspace to be as comfortable as possible for you.

Foods and Drinks

For the seventh chakra, what you'll need are pure foods. As

much as possible, go for organically grown produce. Salads featuring leafy vegetables and homemade dressing are one of the best dishes you can eat for your crown chakra. Prepare your food in colorless glass dining ware, as well. It also helps if you detoxify and fast at least once a year.

Associated Crystals

Amethyst, Moonstone, Labradorite, Sugilite

Amethyst cleanses the aura. It is one of the most spiritual stones, with a high spiritual vibration. It enhances intuition, psychic gifts, spiritual awareness and wisdom. It is a natural tranquilizer and it has a very calming effect on the mind and emotions. Thus, it is effective in the treatment of insomnia. It dispels anxiety, fear, anger and rage. It helps to overcome blockages and addictions (of all kinds). It enhances meditation and a higher state or consciousness. It helps one to understand dreams and enhances visualization. It stimulates the throat and crown chakra. However, this crystal should not be used in cases of schizophrenia and paranoia.

Benefits

It eases headaches, relieves stress, tension, physical, psychological and emotional pain. It cleanses the blood. It reduces swelling and bruising. It enhances the metabolism and endocrine system. It heals various diseases of the lungs and respiratory tract, the digestive system, cellular disorders, as well as skin conditions. It alleviates grief and sadness.

Placement

You may wear this as jewelry, especially over the throat or heart. You may place geodes or clusters in your home. You may place it under your pillow to ease insomnia. Single points are usually used for healing. It will fade if placed in the sun.

Protection

It is an extremely protective stone. It has strong cleansing and healing powers. It blocks negative environmental energies. It protects against recurrent nightmares. It promotes love of the divine and encourages selflessness.

Source

Brazil, Sri Lanka, Mexico, Canada, East Africa, Uruguay, India, Russia, Britain, United States.

Moonstone as its name suggests, is strongly connected to the moon. It is a stone of new beginnings. It enhances psychic abilities. It has a very calming effect and soothes and stabilizes the emotions. Therefore, it promotes deep emotional healing. It eases shock. It is beneficial for hyperactive children.

Benefits

It eliminates toxins from the body and aids in fluid retention. It supports the digestive and reproductive systems. It offers relief for PMS, conception, during pregnancy, during childbirth and breastfeeding. It eases degenerative conditions of the eyes, the hair, the skin, the pancreas, as well as the liver. It may also be used to treat insomnia.

Placement

You may wear it as a pendant or a ring, or place it appropriately on the body. For spiritual experiences, you may place it on the forehead and for emotions, you may place it on the solar plexus chakra or the heart. Women may need to refrain from wearing it during the full moon.

Protection

It calms the emotions, thus it eases overreaction to situations. It is filled with receptive and passive feminine energy. Thus, it balances the male/female energies. In men, it will aid one to get in touch with their feminine side. It is the perfect stone for hyper-masculine men and overly aggressive women.

Source

Australia, India, Sri Lanka.

Labradorite redirects unwanted energies from the aura and serves as barrier to negative energy during energy therapy. It stimulates intuition and psychic gifts and enables access to spiritual purpose. It brings messages from the subconscious to the surface. It calms an overactive mind strengthens the imagination. It enhances introspection. It raises consciousness. It is a stone of transformation and is beneficial to have during times of change.

Benefits

It regulates the metabolism. It reduces stress. It lowers blood pressure, balances the hormones and eases PMS. It can be used to treat disorders of the brain and eyes. It can be used to treat colds and flu, rheumatism and gout.

Placement

You may wear it as a pendant over the heart chakra. You may hold or place it on the body as appropriate.

Protection

It is a protective and mystical stone. It prevents energy leakage from the aura. It dispels fears and insecurities. It eradicates projections and thought patterns of others which have hooded into the aura.

Source

Italy, Finland, Canada, Greenland, Scandinavia, Russia.

Sugilite opens all the chakras. It grounds the soul. It is one of the major "love stones". It enhances spiritual awareness and promotes channeling. It is beneficial when used on spiritual quests and helps to obtain answer to all the important life questions, such as "Who am I?" and Why am I here?" It encourages forgiveness, as well as self-forgiveness. It relieves grief and sorrow.

Benefits

It relieves headaches and pain. It can be used to treat motor disturbances and epilepsy. It aligns the brain and nervous system. It purifies the blood and lymph system. It eases emotional turmoil in cancer sufferers. It can aid people who suffer from schizophrenia and paranoia. It can also aid people who suffer from learning disabilities.

Placement

You may place it on the forehead to ease a headache. You may place it on or over the heart chakra and lymph glands. To alleviate despair, you may place it on the brow chakra (third eye).

Protection

It draws off negative energy. It helps light workers and sensitive people to adapt to the earth's vibrations. It protects the soul from disappointment, shock and trauma. It alleviates spiritual tension. It draws light into the darkest of situations. It can also assist in facing difficult situations.

Source

South Africa, Japan.

Meditation Poses

Savasana (the corpse pose)
- Assume a comfortable lying position. Prior to doing this, it is necessary to regulate the temperature in the room. Do whatever is necessary to provide yourself with comfort. You may place a blanket over yourself or a pillow over your eyes or under your head. To relieve back tension, you may place a

folded towel beneath your knees.

- Make sure that your legs are apart, at least hip width.

- Your arms should be rested on your sides. Ensure that the palms are facing skyward.

- Breathe deeply. Then, tightening your entire body, lift your head off the ground along with your upper and lower extremities.

- Maintain this position for a while. Then, release while breathing out through your mouth.

- Repeat this exercise several times.

- While doing this, envision a violet light shining in your crown chakra. Chant the word "Om".

- Envision a lotus flower on the top of your head. With each inhalation, picture a divine white light pouring into the flower. With every exhalation, imagine all the negativity leaving your body.

- Remain still for at least five minutes and continue your visualization.

- Afterwards, gradually regain your awareness by concentrating on your breath. Reconnect with your physical form by gradually moving your fingers and your toes.

Each time you perform the corpse pose, you are affecting that area of your life which governs your connection with the spiritual realm.

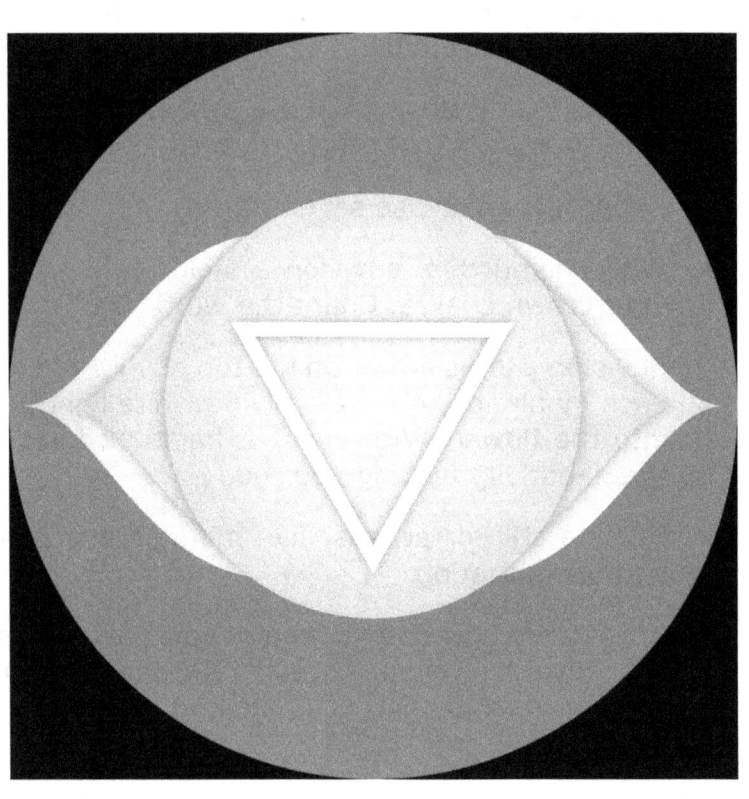

Chapter 2: The Third Eye

Once the creative expression is achieved, spirituality and thoughtfulness become our focus goal. These are just as important to the psyche as basic and social needs, and often provide a deeper, more meaningful purpose to a person's life. When this need is lacking or out of balance, it can have severely detrimental effects, namely a feeling of hollowness, going insane, or troubling confusion.

Located between the eyes and also known as the brow chakra, the chakra is fittingly the center for our sixth sense ("The third eye chakra", n.d.). This is the chakra responsible for our clairvoyance, spirituality, observance, intuition, and instincts. An open third eye will encourage a person to fantasize or daydream in a healthy manner, whereas a mostly closed third eye causes uncertainty, reliance on authority to make decisions, a narrow and stubborn mind not open to new or differing beliefs, and a follower or "sheep in a herd" mentality. Those with an overactive third eye typically wrap themselves in a comforting security blanket of fantasy and imagination, sometimes to the point of hallucinations.

Illusions and misconceived fantasies contribute to the imbalance of this chakra. A person becomes so muddled and caught up in things that aren't real that they practically find themselves trapped inside their own minds. The right to see is violated in this scenario, often discouraging a person from seeking anything outside of the pseudo-safety of their made-up worlds.

Third eye visions are especially vivid and often appear wispy, hazy, or dream-like. As this chakra is related to clairvoyance, clairaudience, and psychic ability, the visions you see during third eye chakra meditations may appear as otherworldly, foreshadowing, or confusing (Luna, 2017). They do not have to make sense right away, simply acknowledge and accept the visions as they come and carry on with your meditation.

At this point in the chakra ladder, opening the third eye will be exceptionally difficult. Dedication and patience are required. It may seem out of reach or impossible, but it can be done in time with practice and focus.

Silence feeds the third eye chakra. It is important to get a bit of time to yourself each day in which your environment is quiet and you are able to engage in either an activity (engaging in archery by yourself, drawing or painting, sculpting, reading, meditation, etc.) or just simply being still and appreciating the lack of noise. A busy, cluttered mind is unable to receive divine messages involving psychic development. Have you ever noticed that many of the mystics or otherwise insightful people you meet tend to be on the quieter side? This is not a coincidence. In order to open the third eye chakra, you must be in tune with the quiet, subtle nature of its frequencies.

While you don't have to become a psychic master by any means, experimenting with tools that exercise your intuition can help strengthen and balance your third eye chakra. Some ways to tap into and build upon your intuitive skills include learning to read tarot cards, observing the moon and being in places where there is moonlight, learning to read palms or tea leaves, respectfully working with spirits and spirit guides, practicing lucid dreaming or astral projection, doing dream work or dream interpretation, meditating, studying symbols around you, nurturing your creativity, and studying astrology and horoscopes (beyond the Western horoscope "readings" one finds on social media, that is). Keeping a dream journal is also encouraged, as dreams are very connected to this chakra and its purpose. This dream journal should describe any dreams you have in as much detail as possible and then include your interpretations of those dreams. These interpretations can be based on your gut feelings, connections between symbols in the dream and your real life, definitions and hints found in dream encyclopedias, and anything else you feel is relevant. Remember that most dreams are not literal, but rather are very metaphorical in nature.

In contrast to this goal of higher wisdom, we must also return to the root chakra and its grounding in order to balance the third eye chakra. Soaring too high and getting your head stuck in the clouds is just as detrimental to your being as going too "low" and not being able to see the metaphysical and mystical at all. As you nurture your intuition and psychic abilities, don't neglect grounding yourself so that you have the strength in foundation to endure the strange and sometimes even unsettling experiences and visions you will have while focusing on activating the third eye chakra. The third eye is not dangerous or evil, but many of us have minds that are not yet used to the information that comes through to us once this chakra has begun to open. This can be shocking and as a result, uncomfortable for some. Thus, it's important to build into it gradually and keep your feet on the ground.

Opening the third eye cannot be done with a mindset of fear. If you convince yourself, as some people do, that the third eye chakra opening and what that entails (the gained visions and insights) are negative and dangerous, you can scare yourself into making that your reality. Nightmares, hallucinations, and mostly negative visions can haunt people who firmly believe that these things will haunt them upon interacting with the third eye chakra. This is only a perception of the mind. Go slowly into opening the third eye and remain grounded. If the experience becomes overwhelming for you, be sure to firmly ground yourself, consider asking spirit guides or angels to protect and aid you, praying, burning sage smudges, or anything else you know makes you feel more protected and secure.

Causes of Blockage

There are a number of elements that could be blocking your third eye chakra. Primary among them are issues of overwhelming grief and emotional pain. Severe trauma can indeed blind your third eye, but there are some other potential outlying causes to be concerned with as well.

Here are some potential direct causes:

- Use of Fluoride

Here is a case in which the physical world has a direct impact upon a chakra. In this case the fluoride contained in the regular, everyday tap water that we drink has a toxic effect on the pineal gland, which in essence is the third eye's physical representative. It is said that phosphate from fluoride can accumulate in the pineal gland over time and cause the gland to harden and be less effective. This buildup will disturb—among other things—the production of melatonin, an important relaxing agent which aids in the process of sleep. And any time you mess with the body's ability to sleep, the chakric system takes a direct hit. Be very careful about the use of fluoride.

- Overuse of Health Supplements

Most of us probably do not see any harm in taking health supplements whatsoever, but there is indeed a downside when it comes to affecting your chakras, including the third eye chakra. Of particular note is mercury. Supplements heavy in mercury tend to have a direct effect on your chakras. Always be careful not to overuse health supplements.

- Subconscious Self-Blockage

This one gets us into the metaphysical realm. According to the proponents of subconscious self-blockage, one reason why the third eye can be blinded, is that someone has seen something in the astral realm—something supernatural, and they weren't quite prepared for what they saw. Supposedly the shock of this event for the uninitiated was so great that their subconscious mind willfully chose to block out the event from memory. And as this self-defense mechanism played out, their third eye chakra was completely shut down as a result. Now what the shocking supernatural event that they witnessed was remains open to conjecture, but whatever it was that they saw gave them the heebie-jeebies so bad that they willfully slammed the lids on their third eye shut through a subconscious self-blockage of their chakra.

- Being Subjected to Vocational Criticism

It may seem like a minor thing but when someone attacks your livelihood they are essentially attacking your purpose in life and such barbs can do more damage to our psyche than we might realize at the time. Being subjected to vocational criticism can indeed cause our third eye chakra to close up. If we feel our vision of the future is being overly criticized, we might choose to close our eyes altogether.

Symptoms of a Blocked Chakra

Symptoms of a blocked third eye chakra tend to stand out. They have many physical manifestations that are disruptive in our day to day routine life. We will discuss a few of the most common in further detail below.

- Lack of Direction

Disrupted third eye chakra's can—and often does—disrupt one's feeling of direction in life. When there is blockage in third eye chakra, you can feel as if your internal compass has been turned off. With the energy center of this chakra wearing thin you may also find yourself wary of even your own conscious. Losing all sense of what is right and wrong. All human beings on this planet need to have an easily definable purpose and without it we are indeed pretty lost. Having a lack of proper direction can be absolutely devastating to your chakra.

- Fearful Outlook

Being constantly fearful is a horrible way to have to live life, but when the chakra is blocked, the fear experienced could become overwhelming. Someone who has this issue with their chakra might find themselves constantly creating negative thought patterns about themselves and the world around them. They feel that everyone is judging them and ready to pounce, and fear making a move lest they step on an eggshell. It is a precarious position to be in, but thankfully there is a way out. Follow the guidelines presented in this chapter to break out of this fearful state of being.

- Inability to Concentrate

Having a hard time concentrating is a direct consequence of having a blocked third eye chakra. The chakra is all about "manifesting our desires". But when this chakra is blocked, our concentration can quickly go astray. So, if you are having a distinct difficulty in holding your concentration this could be a clear sign of an interruption of the flow of energy to and through your third eye chakra.

- Chronic Depression

Chronic depression can cause a lot of problems, and when the chakra is blocked it becomes all-pervasive throughout the individual's life. All creativity and willpower can become submerged into a dark cloud of depression if the chakra is not effectively brought back to a place of equilibrium. Clinical depression is indeed a chronic issue, and it is even more troubling with a blocked chakra.

- Severe Headaches

Having a really bad headache, especially migraine-type headaches centered around the forehead and between the eyes are an indication of a third eye chakra run amok. The third eye is located in this region, and any chronic physical manifestation of pain could be representative of a deeper discord with the chakra.

- Eye Problems

If you are suffering from various eye problems your blocked chakra could be responsible. These problems can range from slightly blurred vision all the way to blindness. There are many cases of those suffering from various conditions of the eye going into instant remission as soon as their ailing chakra was tended to.

- Nightmares

Nightmares are the result of accumulated fears, doubts, and worries. And if your chakra is malfunctioning, these elements can accumulate in the mind, leading to many bad dreams down the road. The chakra is said to rule over our sleeping state, and if you are getting spooked by things that go "bump in the night" you just might blame it on your unbalanced third eye chakra.

- Insomnia

Just like the nightmares mentioned above, insomnia could become another bedfellow of those with a misaligned chakra. In order to get the rest that you need, you will have to address the problems in your chakra.

- Feeling Disconnected

When your third eye chakra is disconnected, you yourself might indeed feel completely disconnected from the world around you. Your third eye chakra is meant to be your all-seeing guide, but when it has been blinded you become like a ship without a compass.

Ways to Open this Chakra Back Up

This chakra is very sensitive, and some would even say clairvoyant in scope. But once this delicate piece of chakric equipment breaks down, it can be very troubling. Fortunately for us—there are however, quite a few methods at our disposal to use to open it right back up again.

And these include:

- Mindful Meditation

In order to practice mindful meditation for this chakra, you need to find a quiet place where you can relax, let go, and be yourself. Sit down either on a cushion or the bare floor/ground below you and begin taking long deep breaths. Now visualize your third eye chakra, located just above your nose and right in the middle of your forehead. Envision this chakra opening up as you continue to breathe in deep. As you picture the chakra opening up, imagine the energy of this chakra coursing through your body more and more with each and every breath. By the time you are through, your chakra will be wide open once again.

- Repeat Positive Mantras

Mantras seek to flip the script when it comes to negative thinking. They are used to reverse negative thoughts with the power of positive affirmations. This change in direction is often crucial in opening up a blocked chakra. A few examples of positive mantras are, "I follow the lead of my inner self" and "I am on my true path." Repeat these positive mantras just a few times, and you will soon see the difference as your third eye responds in kind.

- Connect with Nature

Sometimes something as simple as taking a walk in the park can do wonders for opening up a closed-off chakra. Nature takes us back to our initial love of creation, helping us tap into the universal love that is there for us all. Connect with nature and your chakra will receive the boost it needs to get itself back online.

- Use Your Creativity

Also, doing creative activities such as playing music, painting, or writing can help you spark the creative and intuitive power that resides within your third eye chakra. If you are facing a blocked chakra, don't hesitate to use your creativity.

- Adjust Your Diet

In general, if you wish to have a healthy chakra system you need to eat a balanced diet with plenty of fruits and veggies. But even more than this, when it comes to this chakra, there are certain foods that can enhance the ability of this energetic circuit more than others. Dark chocolate, for example, is great for helping people to concentrate, which is tremendously beneficial when it comes to focusing on clearing your chakra circuit. Another good dietary choice would be walnuts and salmon, as these super foods are loaded with omega-3 which is another booster of cognitive function that can help you better prepare the opening of your blocked chakra. Adjust your diet and you can adjust the entire outlook of your third eye.

Signs and Symptoms of Awakening the Third Eye

Awakening of the third eye is a mystical phenomenon. Some people get the realization immediately and others may not feel it so vividly. However, the signs are visible to everyone. The need is to look closely and feel them. One of the best impacts of the opening of the third eye is the supreme calm and relaxation the experience offers. The person whose third eye has awakened will have a feeling of higher self and a better control of heart and mind. There are several short and long-term signs that start appearing as the third eye awakens. However, the experiences and appearances of these signs may differ from person to person.

An individual may not feel all the symptoms but, even if some of the symptoms arise you must understand that your third eye has awakened. You must continuously work towards opening it. Meditation gives you greater power and control over it. It uplifts you. It infuses a feeling of higher self. Your consciousness broadens. Your mind awakens to a new light. You will start feeling calm and composed. This power doesn't give you victory over others but victory over yourself. It lets you control your desires and aspirations. It makes you understand the futility of most of the aspirations in life. Material gains hold very little importance for the awakened individual. You will become more content and blissful.

Awakening of the third eye can also bring intense physical sensations. These sensations are very clear. If you feel any of these, then you must know that your third eye has started opening. You must work harder towards understanding it and using it for the good of everyone. It isn't just a power or achievement. It is the gift of nature to you that can be used for the greater good of humanity.

There may be several short-term signs of the third eye awakening.

Some of the Short-Term Signs are:

☐ **Tingling Sensation**

You may feel a tingling sensation on your forehead. This is unmistakable. You may try to brush it off involuntarily several times. It is a feeling of strange cold on the forehead. It is the effect of that cold eternal light. It is intense but not hot. It has a very soothing effect on you. But in the beginning, you may find it strange.

☐ **Pressure**

You may feel some pressure at the focus point.

In the initial stages, you may feel a strange pressure on your focus point. This also happens in the initial stages when the third eye starts to awaken. It is a basic form of resistance. Pressure on your focus point is a good sign. It means that you are making progress in your endeavors.

☐ **Headaches and Vivid Dreams**

This sign can scare some people. You may experience headaches or a feeling of drowning at some stage of the meditation. There are several reasons for it. When you go toward the light, there is a vast expanse. It is a bottomless pit. You may feel that you are falling and drowning in it. But, you cannot drown. It is engulfing you. It is testing you as you are testing it. There is no reason to fear it. You need to embrace it. Some people can also experience vivid dreams and nightmares. It happens when you still have insecurities, fears, and worries. These are all negative energies and they try to drag you into the darkness. There are all kinds of energies around us. The positive as well as the negative energies. They are in constant conflict. If you tend towards negative energies then they may try to take control of you. Scare you from your path. You only need to be strong and determined. If you remain firm and focused, these symptoms will vanish.

☐ **Emotional Outbursts**

Emotional strength is very important on this path. Awakening the third eye is a very overwhelming experience. It is the path of self-introspection. The karma will come in front of you. You will become answerable to everything you have ever done. There is no outward appearance here. You can't blame others for these actions and outcomes. It can become a very emotional journey. This is among the reasons that it is advised to leave your emotions and feelings behind before you embark on this journey. It is not a lie detector test that you can bypass. Here, the truth itself will face you. You may feel overwhelmed at times.

The failure to awaken the third eye also leads to emotional outbursts in some people. There is no reason for that. You are the only one responsible for success or failure on this path. You must remember that you are walking on it all alone. Even greatest of the gurus will leave you at the beginning of the journey. They can only show you the path. No one walks the path for you. If you fail, keep trying. Winning control of the emotions is very important. Still, if after the sessions you feel that you have started showing the signs of having emotional outbursts, then you must understand that you are in the process of awakening the third eye. You are fighting the final battle. It is a sign.

☐ **Seeing Colors**

Some people may also see rainbow colors during meditation and even with their eyes open. There is no reason to worry about that. It is the third eye awakening. It may project various colors and shapes in front of your eyes. It will subside after some time. You are on the right track and there is no reason to worry.

Long-Term Signs

☐ **Increased Awareness**

You will become more aware and alert. You might catch even those details that are not visible in general. You may sense negative and positive energies around you. You may start feeling the vibes coming out of people and things. This is part of your newly gained awareness. It is good. It is your patience, belief, and determination bearing fruit. This awareness is complete. You will become aware of everything, including your actions and the actions of others.

☐ **Your Intuition Will Improve Significantly**

The third eye bestows the power of intuition. You will become more intuitive. Your decision-making process will improve. You will know about the good and the bad by observing their auras. It is the guiding light. You will make correct decisions. There will be a force stopping you from taking the wrong path. A power that tells that something wrong is about to happen. This is the biggest gift of the third eye.

☐ **You Will Feel Whole with Your Being**

There will be no emptiness. There will be no conflict. You will not remain indecisive. You will become complete. You can never feel lonely. Your soul will become activated. It will become your companion. You will embrace everything in this universe. The feelings of contempt and pride will diminish. You will know that there is nothing superior or inferior in this world.

☐ **Your Psychic Visions Will Improve**

You will be aware of the otherworldly impressions. This can work as a positive as well as a negative thing for some people. Your encounters with the unworldly beings and powers may increase. They may not have any power over you but they may be able to interact with you. This scares some people. There is nothing to worry about, but some people may feel afraid of this power. But once you have started on this path, there is no going back. You can't undo what has been done. You will have to learn to embrace this power.

These are all signs that your third eye has awakened. But, the third eye awakening is not just about powers and signs. It is more about realization. You will have a greater and clearer self-realization. Before you can have any impact on others, you will have a greater impact on yourself. It is a gift. A gift no one else can give you. It is the fruit of your determination. You will have to learn to accept it and use it for the greater good of your fellow human beings.

Foods and Drinks

Freshwater fish like eel, carp, dace, tench, bass, trout and catfish are among the best foods for your third eye chakra. Reap the most benefits out of these foods by preparing them right after you catch them.

Blueberries, blackberries and raspberries are also ideal for your third eye chakra. Mugwort, poppy seed and lavender are great ingredients for your meals if you intend to balance your third eye chakra. Take a sip of grape juice or red wine as well.

Associated Crystals

Apatite, Azurite, Sodalite

Apatite draws off negative energy. It is a good stone for manifestation. It balances the chakras and the physical, mental, emotional and spiritual bodies. It enhances and deepens meditation. It enhances psychic ability. It encourages motivation and openness. It eases sorrow, anger and apathy. It is very beneficial for autistic or hyperactive children. It enhances creativity. It eases emotional exhaustion and expands knowledge and truth.

Benefits

It enhances the body's ability to absorb calcium. It aids the bones, teeth, cartilage, joint health, and improves arthritis and motor skills. It heals bones. It encourages the formation of new cells. It stimulates the metabolism and can suppress hunger. It heals the meridians, glands and organs.

Placement

You may wear it in close contact with the skin, over an affected area or as appropriate.

Protection

It draws off negative energy form oneself and others. It encourages openness, communication, self-expression and extroversion. It disperses confusion and aids in accessing information to be used for the collective good.

Source

Norway, Russia, Mexico, United States.

Azurite cleanses and stimulates the brow chakra (third eye). It raises the consciousness. It facilitates meditation and channeling. It serves as an effective guide in intuitive and psychic development. It encourages enlightenment. It is a powerful healing stone. It eases nervousness. It disperses stress, anxiety, sadness and grief.

Benefits

It relieves stress and encourages mental healing. It detoxifies the body. It heals the liver, gallbladder, kidneys, the teeth, the bones, thyroid, the spleen and the skin. It treats problems with the throat, the joints and arthritis. However, symptoms normally worsen before improvement.

Placement

You may wear it in close contact with the skin on the right side of your body. You may also place it on the third eye or elsewhere upon the body as appropriate. This crystal may cause palpitations, in which case you should remove it immediately.

Protection

It releases blocks in communication. It expands the mind, as it encourages clear understanding. It challenges the mind and assist one in letting go of old belief systems. It dissolves fears and phobias.

Source

Peru, Chile, France, Namibia, Egypt, Russia, Australia, United States.

Sodalite stimulates the brow chakra (third eye). It is an excellent stone for the mind, as it dissolves confusion and encourages intuition, truth, objectivity and rational thought. It opens spiritual perception and filters information from the higher mind into the physical level. It is a very calming stone. It enhances and deepens meditation. It encourages one to stand up for their own beliefs.

Benefits

It enhances the immune system. It can be used to treat the throat, the larynx, the vocal cords, digestive orders and insomnia. It lowers blood pressure and fever. It aids the body in the absorption of fluids. It balances the metabolism. It can help overcome calcium deficiencies.

Placement

You may wear it for long period of time and you may place it anywhere as appropriate.

Protection

It clears electromagnetic pollution. It is an excellent stone to facilitate group work, as it stimulates trust amongst the people in the group. It also encourages interdependence. It is beneficial to people who suffer from "sick-building" syndrome.

Source

Brazil, France, Myanmar, Romania, Greenland, Russia, North America.

Meditation Poses

Sukhasana (the easy pose)

- Assume a sitting position.
- Tuck one heel inward toward your groin. Then, fold the other heel in.
- Perform the hakini mudra. That is, join the fingertips of your right hand with those of your left hand's.
- Close your eyes. Breathe deeply ten times. While doing this, pay attention to the sound of your breathing.
- Each time you breathe in, touch your palate with the tip of your tongue. Then detach it each time you breathe out.
- Afterwards, relax your hands and rest them on your knees.
- Maintain this position for five minutes.
- Meanwhile, imagine an indigo light glowing in your brow chakra. Chant the word "Ohm".

Whenever you perform the easy pose, you are affecting that area of your life which governs your sixth sense. It greatly affects how all of your other chakras function.

Chapter 3: Throat Chakra

Once our basic needs, social place, and deeper bonds are fulfilled, we need to be able to engage in self-expression in order to live a healthy and content life. Suppressing and bottling up emotions, thoughts, and ideas cause a self-destructive effect that drains our psyche and internally frustrates us.

The throat chakra, or vishuddha chakra, represents willpower, wisdom, creative expression, and sincerity (Olesen, 2014). A strong emphasis on truth is placed within this chakra. It connects to the throat, jaw, mouth, and thyroid, and as such when the throat chakra is not properly aligned, it can cause pain and other problems in these areas. Depression is directly linked to the throat chakra, as well as low self-confidence, anxiety, panic, a lack of creative or expressive energy, and aggressive outbursts. Lying and dishonesty further closes this chakra and intensifies many of these problems.

This is the "artist's chakra," the center for creative expression. When it is underactive, artist's block and writer's block may manifest. A person with an underactive throat chakra will often not speak often and come off as very timid, reserved, and caged. Sudden introversion and shyness are sometimes related to this chakra. A person with an overactive throat chakra, on the other hand, tends to speak disproportionately more than they listen. They come off as preachy, self-centered, or inconsiderate to others and tend to have an underlying fear of not being heard.

As this is the chakra of truth and expression, it is violated by lies and dishonesty, either those received or those spoken by the person affected. After a person is constantly lied to or constantly lies, they begin to question their right to hear or speak the truth at all.

The throat chakra can be opened by singing, eating more fruit, and drinking water. Focusing visualization exercises on the associated color blue can also help open this chakra: imagine a radiant, calming blue light, inhale as you visualize health, healing, and blue. Imagine your health and healing being filled with this light, and then exhale, releasing stress with the exhaled breath.

Sound is one of the most powerful sources of energy in the world, and it is very connected to the throat chakra. Speaking positive affirmations, singing, and humming all create vibrational frequencies that will affect you and your chakras. Gossiping, lying, inappropriately speaking, breaking promises, failing to keep secrets, verbal aggression or bullying, and talking more than you're listening are all things to avoid in order to maintain the balance of this chakra. Anything that exercises the use of your vocal chords in a positive manner aids in balancing the throat chakra.

The primary association of the throat chakra, beyond sound, is creative energy and purpose. Your ability to create is a powerful thing, and you do possess that ability – even if your idea of drawing is stick figures or you can't carry a tune, there are far more methods to creation than just these activities. A powerful tool in opening the throat chakra is art journaling. This tool is so useful because it can be adapted to fit anyone, not just professional artists, and is a quick, liberating way to express emotions in a healthy, private manner. Art journals can be created using photographs, illustrations, and drawings, painting, attaching three-dimensional objects (such as ticket stubs, bubble wrap, etc.), magazine clippings, newspaper clippings, stamps, glitter, stickers, and whatever else you feel appropriate. The goal of the art journal is to let go of your inhibitions a bit and let loose onto the paper, freely expressing your thoughts and emotions however you feel you want to. It doesn't have to look pretty or even make sense, it's all up to you. Accepting this chaos and liberating your expression is key to opening the throat chakra.

If an art journal in any form doesn't sound appealing to you, the option of a written journal is also a powerful tool. Being able to privately, freely express yourself in writing without fear of judgment or need for editing is exceptionally liberating.

Write about your experiences, true thoughts, things you might not tell anyone else, things you might not want to particularly tell yourself, your emotions, your ideas, what's going on in your life, what has happened in your life, and anything else you want. There are no rules, the court is entirely yours. Once you have written down how you're feeling, it is typically good practice to read through it again at a later time and evaluate. This often leads to breakthroughs and new realizations.

Realizing your truth and learning to speak openly and honestly is crucial to unlocking the throat chakra. Speaking your emotions to loved ones is often a good place to start. Being able to talk about your thoughts and emotions can be harder than it seems, especially when the throat chakra is still closed, but with some dedication can be done. Once the throat chakra is opened, you will typically have learned how to be open, honest, and sincere in a comfortable, direct way that benefits you well.

Causes of a Bad Throat Chakra

Most of the causes are psychological but there are some instances in which very real physical problems have led to a closed throat chakra, as is the case with an overactive or underactive thyroid. But whether physical or mental, the outcome of a disrupted chakra is the same.

Here is a closer look at some of the direct causes involved:

- Telling Lies

In the world of tabloid media people used to voice the cynical expression, "You should never let the truth get in the way of a good story." But yes, even in today's murky world of fake news, and sensational headlines, telling the truth does still matter. And according to traditional chakric belief, when you tell a pack of lies it can cause a major disruption of your throat chakra. Lies are damaging to both yourself and those around you, but the cumulative effect of all of those lies will be felt by your throat chakra more than anywhere else.

- Being Overly Criticized

If there are those in your life that are overly critical of you, whether it is an overbearing parent, spouse, or friend, they can have a serious impact on your personal esteem and confidence. But much more than that, if the overbearing critic keeps at it, your own personal voice will become so oppressed that your throat chakra will become completely blocked.

- Childhood Trauma

Any significant childhood trauma, whether the abuse afflicted was verbal, physical, or sexual, could have a major impact on the development of your throat chakra. Like the proverbial "lump in your throat" much of the pain and sorrow that we experience in life gets stored in our fifth "throat" chakra. Such situations are understandably difficult to deal with and may take several proactive strategies in order to work through them.

- Overactive Thyroid

Yes, not all causes of a faulty throat chakra are psychological in nature some are indeed physical, as is the case with an overactive thyroid. The thyroid you see is the largest gland in the body and is linked to metabolism, weight, and mood. If your thyroid is out of whack, not only will your throat chakra take a beating, but most likely your entire body. An overactive thyroid should be looked into immediately, not only to open up your throat chakra, but also for the sake of your overall health.

- Not Speaking Up

Many are surprised to hear it, but sometimes not speaking up has consequences. Even though your mother may have often told you, "If you don't have anything good to say, then don't say anything at all," these are not always good words to live by. Sometimes, in certain situations, you have to speak your mind, and let those around you know your opinion. Stifling the strong urge to do so can directly cause a backup or blockage in your throat chakra. If, for example, you see an obvious injustice and stay quiet, the guilt of your silence may linger with you, before it settles into the form of a major blockage of your throat chakra.

- Lack of Forgiveness

Not being willing to live and let live can sap your strength. And a marked lack of forgiveness can lead to a marked blockage of your throat chakra. The bottom line is, none of us are perfect, and we all make mistakes. And those who treat you poorly are not irredeemable, they are simply flawed human beings who need correction. Even so called "bad people" often still have some good in them deep down. The bad apples usually are acting out of ignorance and have no idea the level of harm they are inflicting. Highlighting this fact, we have to look no farther than the example of Jesus Christ on the cross when he cried out, "Father forgive them, they know not what they do!" Many cite this—and rightly so—as a perfect example of forgiveness, but even Christians often miss the point of what Jesus was actually saying. He was looking out at a lost, conflicted, and confused humanity and declaring that they had absolutely no clue what they were doing—if they did, they wouldn't have done it. And that's true for most of us in our day to day interactions. We often hurt each other without even fully realizing the harm we are causing. So, don't let a few of these troubled, confused, and conflicted souls cause you to lose faith in all humanity, and lose your will to forgive. Learn to forgive others as you yourself may someday need to be forgiven, and your throat chakra will always remain open.

Symptoms of a Bad Throat Chakra

There are many symptoms involved with malfunctioning throat chakras, and many of them are physical. Whether you come down with a headache, fatigue, or sore throat, such things could be a direct manifestation of having a blocked throat chakra.

Here are some of the most common symptoms:

- Sore Throat

It may seem rather ironic, but at the same time, rather fitting that a sore throat would accompany an injured throat chakra. It seems that the lump in your throat from too many unresolved conflicts can also metastasize into an etheric blockage of your throat chakra. The throat chakra is associated with your throat as well as your sinuses, mouth, jawline, and thyroid gland. If you are having trouble with any of these, it could be a symptom of an issue with the throat chakra.

- Asthma

The disruption of a malfunctioning throat chakra can present itself in the form of asthma. Just as the energy flow is constricted, the breathing is physically constricted and made more difficult as well. Fittingly enough, breathing exercises have been found to be rather successful when it comes to resolving both asthma and a blocked throat chakra. If you feel your throat chakra is constricted and blocked, the key to unlocking it might be to simply take a few deep, mindful breaths.

- Fatigue

The strain of a blocked throat chakra can lead to chronic fatigue. It is simply exhausting to go through life with such a strain on your center of communication and expression. Every single time you feel stifled or oppressed as an individual it will take a toll on you, and after a while leave you completely exhausted.

- Anemia

Said to be caused by a lack of iron in the blood, anemia can also be instigated by a troubled throat chakra. An unbalanced throat chakra can lead to imbalance throughout the entire body. Someone with such unbalance in their chakric system could find it expressed physically in the form of anemia.

- Fear of Open Discussion

For someone with a blocked-off throat chakra, open discussion is a fearful prospect. They have lost all faith in their own words and ability to speak in front of others leading to great anxiety if they ever have to do so. If you have fear greater than your average stage fright, it could be due to a blocked throat chakra.

- Difficulty of Expression

Someone with a blocked throat chakra may have difficulty expressing themselves. They may have trouble finding the right words since their creative well of expression—their throat chakra—has been effectively blocked off. The throat chakra needs to be kept open and maintained in order to give rise to effective freedom of expression.

- Feeling Misunderstood

Those with a blocked throat chakra often feel misunderstood. The throat chakra, when functioning as it is supposed to, gives us a feeling of connectedness with others, and gives us confidence in our own talents and abilities. But when the throat chakra is blocked, we may feel completely inadequate in expressing ourselves and feel that no one truly understands us.

- Letting Others Carry the Conversation

A blockage of the throat chakra can make one rather timid, and leading the conversation becomes almost impossible for these afflicted individuals. Those who have a blocked throat chakra often find that they have to let others carry the conversation for them. In order to break free from these constraints the throat chakra needs to be opened.

- Being Extremely Non-Confrontational

It's not good to be too confrontational, we hear news reports just about every evening about someone who was just a bit too confrontational—and the outcome usually isn't good. But the other extreme can be just as bad too. Someone who eschews any and all confrontation tends to let others push them around, perpetually stifling their own expression and point of view. And for those that have a disruption of their throat chakra, they can become so non-confrontational in nature that they allow others to walk all over them.

- Lightheadedness

A dysfunction of the throat chakra can lead to feelings of lightheadedness. These feelings of weakness are brought on by the weakened power of the throat chakra. So if you are feeling lightheaded, you may want to take the status of your throat chakra into account.

How to Clear Out a Blocked Throat Chakra

Curing a blocked throat chakra takes a little more than just taking a throat lozenge. But there are some unique ways you can really make a difference.

Try exercises such as:

- Write Yourself Letters

This is another one of those "it may sound silly" types of exercises, but it really is beneficial. Writing letters to yourself can help you loosen and unload baggage that you have been carrying around for some time. It is completely therapeutic in the sense that you can reach right to your inner self and finally work out long-held problems. When it becomes difficult to verbalize how you feel, sometimes writing letters to yourself is a great way to break the ice.

- Speak to Your Inner Child

We all have an inner child, and it needs to be nourished. And in a similar vein to how the above section mentioned writing letters to yourself, you should also attempt to speak to your inner child. It may be an abstract mental exercise, but much of a blocked throat chakra can be alleviated if you would just speak to your inner child in a nurturing manner.

- Yogic Neck Exercises

There are a few really good yoga neck exercises that can be employed to break up blockage of the throat chakra. One of them, called the "neck release movement" involves sitting up straight and moving the neck right to left as you take in long, deep breaths. After doing this for a few minutes, tilt your head toward your left shoulder, and place your left hand on the opposite side of your head. Then repeat this step with your other shoulder. At first, you may feel a little bit awkward getting the movement just right, but soon you will get the hang of it and see great improvement in your throat chakra.

- Meditate in Silence

Sometimes a little silence is really all the doctor ordered, and in the case of the throat chakra, this couldn't be any more true. By meditating in silence, the participant is able to slow down and listen to what their chakra is actually telling them, allowing the blocks that have been placed on their throat chakra to fall away. Find a nice, quiet place to meditate and you will feel all the better for it.

- Breathing Exercises

In order to get your blocked throat chakra back into gear, you can engage in refreshing breathing exercises to open up the obstruction. To do so, get yourself to a comfortable place free of distractions and kneel down onto a cushion or soft carpeting. While kneeling put your hands behind your back and grab onto your ankles. Holding this pose, pull your head back and begin taking long, deep breaths. Do this for a couple of minutes before releasing your grip from your ankles and letting yourself fall forward until the top of your head is touching the floor. Hold this pose for a few seconds before breathing in deeply and reverting back to the original pose to start the breathing exercise all over again. Repeat this exercise a few times or as much as you feel it necessary to do so. As soon as you do, you will begin to notice an almost immediate difference in how you feel.

- Practice Forgiveness

The practice of forgiveness has a direct impact upon our throat chakra, if we can forgive others we can relieve a huge burden from the throat chakra. Bitterness is a plague that can present itself as a direct hindrance to your throat chakra. As mentioned in earlier sections of this book, you really do need to practice forgiveness as much as you can. It doesn't mean that you have to forget grievous harm that has been inflected upon you. If you were carjacked and held at gunpoint it's not expected that you can just willfully wipe that trauma from your memory, but you need to move on as best you can. It's not always easy, but you need to be able to mindfully make the effort to leave the problems of the past in the past, and practice forgiveness in the present.

- Speak Your Mind

As mentioned earlier in this chapter, holding in your commentary when you feel compelled to speak can lead to a blockage of your throat chakra. Not speaking up only leads to regret and suppressed feelings. So, in order to avoid this, be sure to speak your mind when the occasion arises.

- Throat Chakra Stones

As with many other chakras, it has been demonstrated that the placement of throat chakra stones has been able to help open up the pathways of healing for your throat chakra. These stones open up vibrational circuits that are helpful in easing blocked chakras open once again.

- Repeat Positive Mantras

Once again, as is the case with many other blocked chakras, the simple repetition of a few positive mantras can do wonders to restore the flow of energy. Repeat things to yourself such as, "I am free to speak." and "I have a voice." Such phrases are simplistic but effective in opening up the throat chakra.

- Tell the Truth

In the end, one of the best ways of correcting a blocked throat chakra is simply by telling the truth. True words are like nutritious food for our throat chakra and the more it consumes the healthier this chakra is.

Exercises

The best exercise for this region and one that gives instant relief is head rolling. Sit with your spine straight and look to the right, move your head back and rotate it in a counterclockwise motion. Do this slowly and surely rather than rushing at it and then do the same thing in the other direction. You will also get great relief for this chakra by allowing yourself the pleasure of singing. It helps to open up the chakra and at the same time can bring you peace of mind.

Foods and Drinks

Plum and blueberry are two of the best foods for the throat chakra due to their color. Both the throat chakra and the color blue signify trustworthiness.

Fruits like apple, apricot, guava, mango, orange and pear are deemed as foods signifying trustworthiness so they're fit for throat chakra healing, as well. They're considered trustworthy because they often get dropped when they're ripe.

Tangy fruits work wonders for the throat chakra too. These fruits include kiwi, orange, grapefruit and lemon. Salt and lemongrass are the best seasonings for this chakra.

Healing Throat Chakra

When this chakra is blocked, it can cause distress and even illness. When the throat chakra is blocked, you may find you have trouble swallowing and may also suffer from a lot of nervous tension. This section will help you to improve that tension and clear the chakra energy route (Houston, 2019).

Chanting – Although you may have heard of chanting, it's quite possible that you have never taken part in it. Chanting is like singing, but it's a question of singing a word with your lips half closed so that you get a tingle on your lips as you do so. This is a great exercise for opening up your throat chakra as well as working on your third eye chakra.

The kind of word that you can use is "Ohm," and only you can decide the pitch at which you sing the "Ohm" and the amount of time that you hold your breath as you sing it. Try this first. Breathe in and then on the out breath use the chant. Do it over and over again as this helps you to clear that chakra. You can also use this when you meditate, by incorporating the chant into the outward breath.

Joyful singing – You don't have to be a member of the choral society to enjoy this. Simply find a tune that you enjoy singing and sing it ("Know your throat chakra and how to unlock its power", n.d.). Make singing part of your everyday life because when you do, you allow the throat muscles to work and this helps to get rid of the pain in the neck area and to open up the chakra so that your pain levels decrease and you begin to feel more relaxed. There are several reasons why this works. While you are concentrating on something as positive as song, your chakra is not disturbed by your insecurities and worries. Try this in conjunction with mindfulness, and you will be on the road to recovery.

Exercise – There is a wonderful exercise that you can do to help clear the throat chakra. Sit on a hard chair and make sure your feet are grounded and touch the floor. Then you need to place the index finger and the middle finger of your right hand onto the left hand side of the top of your head, bending your head to the side. Breathe in deeply and then when you breathe out feel the air rise to your head's top and tuck the chin in as much as you can. You will feel instant release. Try this exercise several times.

Yoga poses that will help release the throat chakra

These are poses that you will learn easily in the early days of yoga classes, but they are also exercises you can do alone. For these poses, be aware that the manner in which you breathe matters. When you are told to inhale, do so, and when you move during an exhalation, be conscious of the two things coming together. In yoga it is the movement and the breath together that help you to achieve bodily movements and positions that would otherwise be difficult.

Legs up the wall pose

This is a great overall exercise that will help you to open up the throat chakra. Lie on a yoga mat or on a firm bed that is up against a wall, because you need to lie as close as possible to the wall and move your legs upward to be parallel to the wall. Your feet need to be square on to the wall and flat as if you are standing on the ceiling above you. Your arms should be stretched out by your side. Stay in this position for about 10 breaths before releasing yourself and lying flat on the floor with your last exhalation.

A shoulder stand

Lie flat on your back on your yoga mat with your hands by your sides. The legs are lifted into the air so that they form a right angle with the body. Remember, breathe in and move the legs on the exhale. Then take your hands to support your body and lift your torso on the next exhale. Hold this position for several moments before releasing yourself and allowing the body to drop back to the lying down position. Do this several times because with each time that you lift the torso, fresh blood flow to the neck area is possible, thus allowing the muscles in the neck to relax.

The supported fish pose

This is a simple pose but also one that may make you feel

uncomfortable, but you will overcome that feeling as you feel the neck area improving. Roll up a towel into a block and lie this block onto the yoga mat. Be set in a position so that your shoulder blades fall at each side of the block. Then lower your back so that your shoulders are lifted a little. Let your arms drop down at the side and let your head fall back to the mat. This will give your neck the amount of stretch that it needs to open up the chakra. Breathe in and out for about 10 breaths and then as you exhale, lift your body and stretch forward and relax.

The suggestions made in this chapter should help you with one of the most commonly problematic areas of your body. The neck takes on a lot of stress and strain in this modern world. For other chakras, follow the exercises shown in the following chapters.

Associated Crystals

Angelite, Blue Lace Agate, Chrysocolla, Kyanite

Angelite is a stone of awareness. It enhances telepathic communication. It stimulates healing. It helps one to speak your truth. As its name suggests, it facilitates contact with the angelic or ethereal realm. It enhances understanding, acceptance and compassion. It enhances peace and tranquility.

Benefits

It relieves inflammation. It balances the thyroid and parathyroid. It balances the fluids within the body. It repairs blood vessels and tissue. It can cool the skin from sunburn. It can be used to control the weight. It unblocks the energy system and the meridians.

Placement

You may hold or place it on the body as appropriate.

Protection

It offers protection both for people and the environment. It represents peace. It eases psychological pain. It is effective in counteracting cruelty. As it heightens perception and deepens attunement, it makes an ideal stone for healers.

Source

Egypt, Mexico, Peru, Poland, Germany, Britain, Libya.

Blue Lace Agate promotes expression of one's thoughts and feelings and is especially effective in healing the throat chakra. It assists in expressing one's spiritual truth. It links the thoughts to the spiritual vibration. It brings about a feeling of peace.

Benefits

It is very effective in healing the throat, thyroid and lymph infections. It eases problems with the neck and shoulders. It heals fractures, strengthens the skeletal system, it lowers fever, it supports the pancreas. It can be used to treat arthritis and bone deformity. It can be used in sound healing. It can treat brain imbalances, when taken as an elixir.

Placement

Place particularly in the throat area or wherever feels appropriate.

Protection

It dissolves old patterns of suppression and encourages expression, especially in the case where one has a fear of being judged. It neutralizes anger. It assists men in accepting their feelings.

Source

Morocco, Africa, India, Brazil, Unites States, Czech Republic.

Chrysocolla cleanses, calms and reenergizes all the chakras.

It draws off all negative energy. It promotes communication. It enhances self-awareness and inner balance. It promotes truthful communication and inspires creativity. It is a beneficial stone to bring joy into one's life.

Benefits

It strengthens the thyroid and enhances the metabolism. It lowers blood pressure. It aids in healing throat infections, as well as the tonsils. It detoxifies certain organs, such as the kidneys, the liver and the intestines. It balances the blood, provides oxygen to the blood and the cellular structure of the lungs. Thus, it enhances breathing. It regenerates the pancreas and regulates insulin in the body. It strengthens the muscles and eases muscle spasms. It eases menstrual cramps and PMS.

Placement

You may place it on the body as appropriate.

Protection

When placed in the home, it draws off all negative energy. It assists in stabilizing problematic relationships. It reduces mental stress and assists one to accept change. It also encourages inner strength. It helps to overcome phobias and encourages self-awareness.

Source

Mexico, Zaire, Peru, Chile, Russia, United States, Britain.

Kyanite grounds the spiritual energy. It aligns the chakras and subtle bodies. It does not require cleansing, as it does not hold negative energy. It encourages one to speak their truth. It enhances meditation. It encourages intuition and psychic abilities. It disperses stress, anger, frustration and blockages. It encourages dream recall. It instills compassion. It is an excellent crystal for attunements.

Benefits

It eases pain. It lowers the blood pressure. It balances the yin-yang energies. It help to heal infections. It assist in weight loss. It can be used to treat the brain, the thyroid, parathyroid, throat, adrenal glands and the urogenital system. It lowers fever and is beneficial when used for muscular disorders.

Placement

You may wear it as a pendant or place it between the navel and the heart. You may place it on any area where you are experiencing pain.

Source

Brazil.

Meditation Poses

Salamba Sarvangasana (the supported shoulder stand)

- Assume a lying position on a yoga mat. You may support your shoulders by using a folded cloth. Meanwhile, your head should be touching the ground.
- Bend your knees and then sway your hips upward. Position your legs overhead.
- Support the middle part of your back with your hands.
- Lift one of your legs first. Make sure that your toes are pointing skyward.
- Then, maintaining the support on your mid-back, lift your other leg.
- While doing this, pay attention to the way you breathe. Allow your eyes to rest on your chest and watch it rise and fall.

- In your mind's eye, picture a blue-colored light burning in your throat. Chant the word "Ham".

- Maintain this position for up to two minutes.

- Then, you may lower each of your legs one at a time.

Whenever you assume this position, you are affecting that area of your life which governs your personal truths.

Chapter 4: Heart Chakra

Once a person's social needs are met and solidly formed, the next to fulfill is the need for deeper connection and compassion: the need for love, charity, and meaningful bonds with others. The center for love, tolerance, and empathy, the heart chakra is the very core of the soul and is, naturally, found deep within the body's heart. Also known as the anahata, this is the nurturing chakra, responsible for forgiveness, generosity, hope, and compassion ("Know your heart chakra and how to unlock its power", 2018).

An open chakra promotes healthy and happy relationships, friendliness, affection, and a willingness to accept love. When this chakra is underactive, a person becomes cold, detached, and distant from others and often even from themselves. An overactive heart chakra entails a person who is overcompensating with their affections, feels more infatuation than love or (consciously or otherwise) uses what they consider "love" for selfish intentions. Those with this chakra underperforming might have a tendency to come off as overbearing, overly jealous, cold, distant, or insincere to others. Those with a closed heart chakra typically have difficulty maintaining relationships.

The heart chakra is attacked by sorrow and grief. The sadness can develop into a depression, and become so powerful that it convinces the person affected that they do not deserve to love or to be loved, or that they are incapable of feeling or giving love. When this right to love feels as if it has been stolen, a person's life becomes incredibly dim and lonely in more ways than one.

Imbalances in the heart chakra are common to those experiencing the effects of a trauma, handling a recent death of a loved one and the bereavement process, or going through a hard breakup or divorce. Naturally, the heart chakra deals with compassion, love (including self-love), appreciation for beauty, and how we connect to others.

When focusing on the heart chakra, it is imperative to think about our relationships with others. Are the bonds we have with others meaningful and harmonious, or are they strained and shallow? A lot of us have friends we don't even particularly like or "settle" for the company we don't really want to keep, and this can be connected as a matter of an imbalance in the heart chakra. Learning to value others and working at our relationships (platonic, romantic, and otherwise) comes with learning to value ourselves and work at that relationship first. "Love yourself first" is an overused phrase many of us are tired of hearing, or the ever-popular and somewhat damaging to hear "No one will love you until you love yourself." While this isn't exactly true, respecting yourself and being able to establish healthy boundaries will result in much better, more stable, less selfish relationships. We don't want to suffocate others or become codependent, but we don't want to lock ourselves away from connection either, however intimidating it may be. In most scenarios, there is a root cause as to why we are especially withdrawn from others or especially dependent on them, why we seek the relationships and the people we do (be they good or bad), and why we feel a certain way about ourselves.

Stopping to "smell the roses" and appreciate the aesthetic beauty around us encourages an open heart chakra. Surround yourself with things you find beautiful, dress in clothing that makes you feel good about yourself, buy yourself a piece of jewelry or flowers, light candles, or place appealing decorations around the home. Enhancing your environment allows the heart chakra room to grow and flourish. Going somewhere you can appreciate art (a museum, a park, a theater or concert, etc.) is another way to begin healing this chakra. Your body is also one major point of beauty you'll want to pay extra attention to – run yourself a warm bath with rose petals, take a little extra time on your appearance in the morning, have your hair or nails done for you, whatever makes you feel good about yourself and nurtures and praises your body.

Do your relationships support you and help you grow? Some

friendships and bonds really do turn into nothing more than dead weight over time. If you feel disrespected, ignored, unappreciated, ridiculed, or undervalued by the people around you, it just might be time to either work it out or to walk away. Surround yourself with people willing to work things through, admit their mistakes, and grow along with you. Give less of your energy to those who insult or belittle you or make you feel like you are not enough. In healthy relationships, you should never be made to feel like you are not worthy or insignificant. Relationships should be balanced, harmonious, and include mutual bonds with respect, compassion, and empathy. You owe it to yourself to accept no less, and your heart chakra picks up on this right away.

Though messy and sometimes incredibly challenging, especially if you have experienced a great deal of trauma or heartbreak in the past, in order to open the heart chakra, you must address and thoughtfully reflect on your past relationships and how they have affected you. This includes family relationships and going back to your childhood in many cases. In working to come to terms with your past relations, you should consider forgiveness and empathy. Despite what some may tell you, forgiveness is not always possible or realistic. If you are unable to forgive those who have wronged you in serious ways, you must still work to forgive yourself and release your heart from any feelings of guilt or self-blame.

Of course, the heart chakra goes beyond just you and your relationships. Transcending ego is helpful in unblocking the heart chakra. This can be done by opening yourself up beyond your immediate personal life, paying attention to and accepting the world outside, your community and other communities beyond it. Balancing the heart chakra entails learning to keep an open mind and treating all people and events with compassion in the foreground, while remaining open to receiving and giving love. Community service is often a great place to start building or nurturing this compassion while at the same time giving back to the world around you. There are community service opportunities everywhere around you, including those done entirely from home, those with very relaxed time commitments, and those that work more closely with nature, art, or animals rather than people (this can be a good place to start if you suffer from social anxiety or aren't especially comfortable around people just yet). If you lean towards being a giving person and self-sacrifice, focus more on accepting love and care from yourself and others, rather than being the source of care for everyone else most of the time. And vice versa, if you lean towards being more of a taker rather than a giver, focus more on giving to others and expressing generosity.

Expressing gratitude directly feeds the heart chakra. As such, take count of your blessings, make a list of everything in your life that you are thankful for, and note all the things you love about your friends and the people around you. Look for the good in others, look for people doing good things for each other and having each other's backs. Allow acceptance and love to grow in your heart, allow your love to thrive and avoid becoming bitter, despite any negative experiences or the ugly things you might see in the world today.

Exercises

This is an important chakra and one that can really make a difference to your happiness in life. Therefore, the exercises here are advised for everyone. You can never have too much love in your heart. The best exercise you can use to heal this chakra is to be more aware of others, to learn empathy and to learn humility. When you are able to open up your heart to others, you will find that you gain a great sense of well-being. Be honest and loving and have a smile for people, even when they don't particularly merit it. It's healing for the heart and helps you to move past periods of negativity. If you are looking for a yoga style that will help the heart chakra, then the ideal is hot yoga (otherwise known as Bikram Yoga).

Foods and Drinks

Green foods suit the heart chakra. Aside from having the associated color for the said chakra, Chinese beliefs suggest that green fruits and vegetables are neutral, as they're neither yin nor yang. This makes them a great chakra-balancing food for the middlemost energy center.

These include leafy vegetables like broccoli, spinach, kale, lettuce and cabbage. Cucumber, asparagus, Brussels sprouts, kiwi, avocado, lime, bell pepper, green peas and green olives are also ideal for the fourth chakra. Parsley, cilantro, basil, thyme and sage are among the spices that can be healing for your heart chakra.

Eating with your loved ones can boost the positive energy in your heart chakra. If you're stressed out, avoid munching because the food you're eating may become comfort food. You may end up depending on it for stress relief. While this may be helpful and not that damaging in the short term, this can make you forget about relieving your imbalanced chakras and prompt you to focus on temporary and ineffective treatments.

Associated Crystals

Moss Agate, Pink Calcite, Rhodonite, Rose Quartz

Moss Agate is highly linked with nature and therefore has a stabilizing effect on the energy. It reduces sensitivity to environmental pollution and extreme weather. It serves as an aid for midwives. It releases blockages and is beneficial to new beginnings. It enhances intuition. It promotes communication and self-expression. It is helpful in treating depression.

Benefits

It enhances the immune system. It cleanses the circulatory system. It has anti-inflammatory properties. It prevents dehydration and hypoglycemia. It can be used to treat colds, flu, (low) fever and infection. It treats skin infections. It speeds up recovery and reduces the risk of long term illness.

Placement

You may hold or place this appropriately in contact with the skin.

Protection

It reduces stress and feelings of fear. It enhances one's ability to get along with other people. It improves the self-esteem and enhances ones positive traits. It gives insight into difficult situations.

Source

Australia, India, United States.

Pink Calcite cleanses negative energy from a room. It dissolves stagnant energy. It is linked to the higher consciousness. It promotes forgiveness and releases grief and fear from the heart. It enhances feelings of self-acceptance and self-worth. It reduces anxiety and tension.

Benefits

It enhances the immune system. It prevents blood clots and stimulates healing tissue. It enhances the body's ability to absorb calcium and dissolves calcifications. As an elixir, it works effectively when applied to the skin. It eases intestinal conditions. It dissolves resistance and heals nervous conditions.

Placement

You may wear it as a pendant. You may hold or place it as appropriate. You may use it in a crystal grid around your bed. You may use it as an elixir.

Source

Belgium, Brazil, Peru, Iceland, Romania, United States, Britain, Slovakia, Czech Republic.

Rhodonite grounds the energy and clears and activates the heart chakra. It balances the emotions and heals emotional shock. It promotes forgiveness and assists in reconciliation. It integrates the physical and mental energies. It enhances confidence. It clears away past emotional wounds, resentment and anger. It enhances mantra-based meditation.

Benefits

It can be used to treat inflammation in the joints, stomach ulcers, emphysema, multiple sclerosis and autoimmune disease. It relieves pain and irritation from insect bites. It aids in healing wounds, it reduces scarring and promotes growth of the bones. It fine-tunes auditory vibrations and hearing. It increases fertility. For the treatment of shock or trauma, it is effective as an elixir.

Placement

You may place it on the skin, to heal internal or external wounds. You may place it on the heart chakra to heal emotional wounds or place as appropriate.

Protection

It balances the emotions. It allows one to see both sides of a situation or issue. It is beneficial in the treatment or prevention of codependency, emotional self-destruction and abuse.

Source

Brazil, Mexico, Spain, Germany, Sweden, Russia.

Rose Quartz is the stone of unconditional love. It opens and purifies the heart on all levels. It enhances self-love and inner healing on a much deeper level. It also encourages self-forgiveness. It assist greatly in situations of crisis or trauma. It opens one up to receiving love. It comforts in time of grief. It is one of the optimum healers.

Benefits

It increases fertility. It strengthens the heart and the circulatory system. It heals the adrenals and the kidneys. It aids in the treatment of chest and lung problems (when placed on the thymus). It is helpful in the treatment of senile dementia, Parkinson's and Alzheimer's disease. It releases impurities from the body's fluids. It alleviates lightheadedness.

Placement

You may wear this in close contact to the skin. You may wear it on the heart, or the thymus. You may place it in the "relationship corner" of a room.

Protection

It instils the true essence of love. When placed next to your bed or in the "relationship corner" of your home, it may attract love. It promotes acceptance of change. It strengthens sensitivity and empathy. It releases emotional heartache.

Source

South Africa, Brazil, Madagascar, India, Unites States, Japan.

Meditation Poses

Ustrasana (the camel pose)

- Position yourself on your knees. Ensure that the space between your knees is as wide as your hips.
- Sit back on your heels.
- Then, position your hands so that they are on your chest.
- Tuck your toes. Ensure that the space between your toes is as wide as your hips.

- Lift yourself so that your hips are brought over your knees.

- Afterwards, position your palms on the lower part of your back. Make sure that your fingers are pointed upwards. As you do this, move your sacrum downwards while lifting your frontal hip bones upward.

- Lean backwards with your head tilted and hyperextended. Touch your heels with your hands. Prior to arching back, think of someone or something that you love. Dedicate this movement to that person or that object.

- Maintain that position while breathing in a relaxed manner.

- As you are doing this, imagine that your heart chakra is radiating a green light. Chant the word "Yam".

- Take some deep breaths and then realign your head with your sacrum. Sit on your heels. You may resume your original hand position by joining them together on your chest. Bow your head.

Whenever you exercise this pose, you are affecting that area of your life which governs love. The camel pose will enable you to heal old emotional wounds and open up your heart.

Chapter 5: Solar Plexus Chakra

Once a sense of happiness is found, people typically feel a need for those with which they can share it. Socializing is a human need, and even the most introverted person is no exception to this. A good part of our sense of purpose comes from how we are established among our social groups. Also known as the manipura or navel chakra, the solar plexus is in charge of the confidence and sense of control that relates to our social standing, our willpower, and our personal power ("Things you should know about the solar plexus chakra", 2018). It places emphasis on self-esteem and how we feel about ourselves when we interact with ourselves and others. When balanced, you feel confident and in control. When this chakra underperforms, you might not have found the voice to speak up for yourself, you let things slide even if they're unfair to you because you don't want to be a burden, and you tend to be indecisive and passive. In contrast, an overactive solar plexus creates an abrasive, pushy, and often aggressive person.

Overpowering shame can bring on issues in the solar plexus chakra. This shame becomes so paralyzing to those affected that it can rob a person of feeling they have the right to act. Every action that person makes becomes unsure and internally over-scrutinized. This presents itself in one of two ways: over-compensated arrogance, or crippling insecurity.

The solar plexus is opened when we are assertive and feel powerful in ourselves. When we walk with an air of power about ourselves, the solar plexus is typically in good standing and we tend to see better results in life because we are actively demanding those results. Learning to say no when you want to or need to, developing a healthy respect for yourself, and learning that you cannot help others before you help yourself (after all, you cannot pour from an empty cup) are all important aspects of coming to a point psychologically where your solar plexus chakra can be opened.

Issues with authority tend to connect to an unbalanced solar plexus. Getting a solid handle on balancing your self-esteem can be a trying period to get through emotionally, but it is necessary in order to balance the solar plexus and to be sincere with yourself. When you're focusing on opening and balancing the solar plexus chakra, it might be good practice to leave motivational, encouraging notes around your home and car. Positive affirmations, feel-good quotes, photos that make you feel joyful, and anything else that brings you a sense of confidence can be left in places you'll see often. You can place them on mirrors, inside a planner or book you read often, or as notes on your cell phone.

Meditation practices are especially effective in activating the solar plexus chakra. Imagine a glowing ball of golden light similar to a tiny sun, a brightly burning fire, or a glowing golden flower during these meditative practices.

The solar plexus chakra is highly related to fire and the sun, so getting plenty of sunlight plays a part in healing and charging this chakra. Lighting candles, being near a bonfire or other flame, being surrounded by warmth (an electronic heating pad or heated blanket is ideal if you do not already live in a naturally warm climate) and sunbathing when possible help open the solar plexus. People are designed to need sunlight in order to absorb the proper nutrients in the body and to maintain a healthy mental state void of depression, so it's no wonder sunlight is also a need demanded by our chakra system. Night shift workers and those who spend most of their time in the dark or up at night tend to have imbalances in their solar plexus chakra because of this. You do not have to adapt your lifestyle to be more daytime-friendly and full of light if this the case, so long as you address the deep-rooted, long-term causes of the unbalance. These deep-rooted causes, as far as the solar plexus goes, generally have something to do with your ego and self-confidence.

Exercises

You may have trouble believing this exercise works, but it really does. Dance and get your hips swinging. I told this to one lady who came to me for help and not only did it help her with her self-esteem issues, but she also started to take a course so that she could teach people the same dancing methods. She lost weight, she gained confidence and at the same time, her chakra healing helped her to enjoy her life to the fullest. This is the easiest form of exercise for people, even for those with little or no experience with yoga. Use Zumba videos from places like YouTube and just let it all hang out. As far as yoga exercises are concerned, the ideal exercise for this region of the body is the boat pose. Lie flat on the floor and then lift your body with your arms stretched forward at the same time as lifting your legs.

Foods and Drinks

Dairy products like cheese, milk and yogurt suit the needs of the third chakra. Consume cereals, breads and pastas, as well. Spice up your meals and beverages using mint, ginger, cumin, turmeric and chamomile to balance this energy center.

Yellow fruits like banana, mango, pineapple and pear are your best choices for your solar plexus chakra. As for savory and spicy dishes, you can prepare and eat a heartful of traditional curry. This is probably the most well-known Indian dish. Curry reminds you of empowerment thanks to its strong flavors.

Associated Crystals

Aragonite, Citrine, Tigers Eye, Yellow Jasper

Aragonite centers and grounds physical energy. It deepens one's connection to the earth. It stabilizes spiritual development. It draws energy into the body and assists in meditation. It enhances concentration, flexibility and tolerance. It restores balance.

Benefits

It enhances the body's ability to absorb calcium. It heals bones and restores elasticity to the discs. It strengthens the immune system, and regulates the body's processes. It eases muscle spasms, alleviates pain, it treats chills and is effective in the treatment of Reynaud's disease.

Placement

You can wear it as a pendant, or placed underneath a pillow. It may be held or placed over an affected part of the body. One may also add this as an elixir to the bath.

Protection

It instills acceptance and patience. It is an effective crystal for people who tend to push themselves too hard. It encourages reliability and discipline. It reduces stress and anger. It assists one in getting to the core of problems.

Source

Namibia, Spain, Britain.

Citrine is an environmentally protective crystal. It absorbs, grounds and dissolves negative energy. It cleanses the chakras and protects the aura. It does not need cleansing. It enhances intuition. It cleanses and balances the subtle body and realigns it with the physical body. It enhances creativity.

Benefits

It stimulates various bodily functions and organ systems, such as the spleen, the digestive system, and the pancreas. It aids in combatting infection in the bladder and kidneys. It detoxifies the blood, increases blood circulation, balances the thyroid and activates the thymus gland. It is also helpful in the treatment of eye problems, menstrual problems and constipation. It balances the hormones, reduces hot flashes and eases menopause.

Placement

You may wear this in close contact with the skin. You may also wear it near the throat or on the fingers. Otherwise, you may place it appropriately on the body.

Source

France, Brazil, Madagascar, United States, Britain, Russia.

Tigers Eye draws spiritual energies to the earth and creates a high vibrational energy, by combining the energies of the sun and the earth. It stimulates the lower chakras. It grounds the energy, fixes change onto the physical body and aids in manifestation. It enhances perception. It alleviates depression. It promotes feelings of self-worth.

Benefits

It heals the throat and the reproductive organs. It dissolves constrictions within the body and enhances night vision. It aids in the healing process of broken bones. It aids in healing personality disorders and mental illnesses.

Placement

You may wear it as a pendant or on your right arm. You may place it on the navel to assist in grounding the chakric energy. You may place it on the body as appropriate. It should, however, not be worn for long periods of time.

Protection

It is a protective crystal. It protects against ill wishes. It enhances psychic ability. It encourages integrity. It promotes clarity and intention.

Source

South Africa, Mexico, Australia, India, United States.

Yellow Jasper stimulates the solar plexus chakra. It grounds and protects the energy. It aligns the chakras. It balances the yang and yin energies. It aligns etheric realm elements like mental, physical, and emotional bodies. It facilitates in dream recall and shamanic journeys. It is supportive during stressful times and reminds people to help one another.

Benefits

It energizes the endocrine system. It releases toxins from the body and heals stomach and digestive problems. It eases pain. It channels positive energy, thus promoting a feeling of physical well-being.

Placement

As it works slowly, you may use it for long periods of time. It may be in close contact with the skin. You may place it on the chest, throat, forehead or wrist. You may also place it on any area where you are experiencing pain.

Protection

It protects during travel and spiritual work. It absorbs negative energy and cleanses the chakras and aura. It clears environmental and electromagnetic pollution, as well as radiation. It has a very calming effect on the emotions.

Source

Worldwide.

Meditation Poses

Navasana (the boat pose)

- Assume a sitting position with your legs placed in front of you.

- Draw your knees towards your chest. Afterwards, support the back part of your knees so that you are able to lift your feet off the ground and balance yourself while you are seated on your ischium.

- Make sure that your chest is lifted while your shoulders are down. The weight must be distributed forward, towards the front of your ischium while you are pulling your navel inwards. Doing this will help to strengthen your core muscles.

- Stretch your arms forward while holding your legs up high.

- As you breathe out, cross your upper extremities around your chest. Then, gradually lower your inferior extremities but make sure that they do not completely touch the floor. Lower your legs just enough so that they are a few inches off the floor.

- Then, breathe in. As you do this, gradually resume the boat position.

- Keep doing this up to five times.

- Afterwards, you may lie down on your back.

- While performing this exercise, visualize the color yellow flaring from your solar plexus chakra. Then, chant the word "Ram".

Whenever you practice this position, you are affecting that area of your life which governs productivity and self-esteem. This will help prevent fear and stagnation in life.

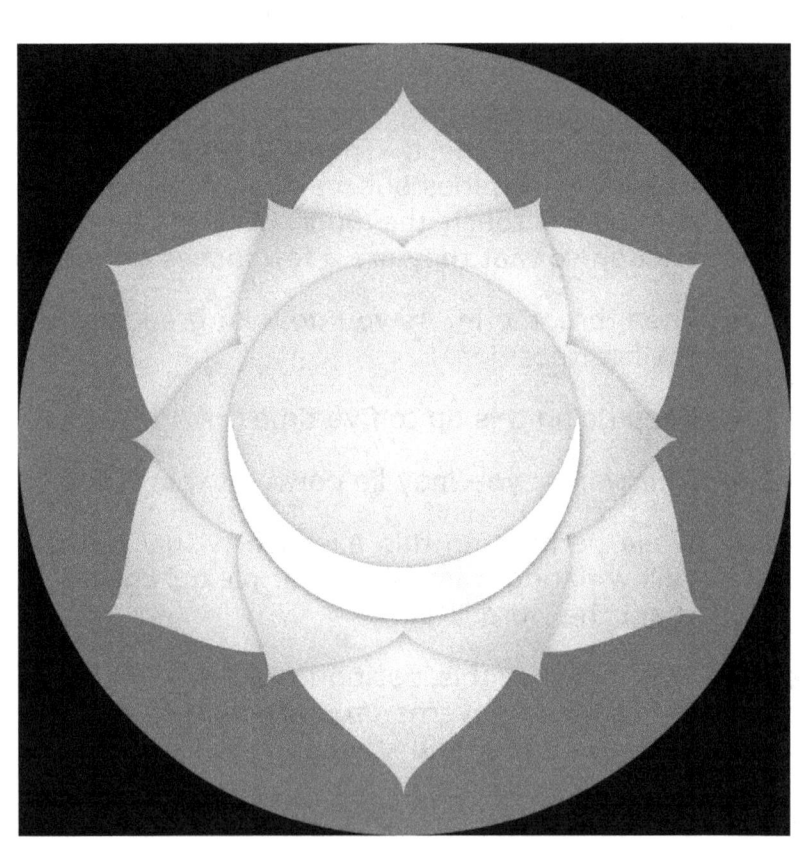

Chapter 6: Sacral Chakra

Once a person's base survival needs are met, the pursuit of joy is usually next on the ladder to personal fulfillment. The sacral chakra of passion, emotion, intimacy, and pleasure is located in the pelvic area and builds off of the first chakra's survival focus by desiring, now, joy.

While the sacral chakra is sometimes referred to as the spleen chakra, there is some confusion surrounding terms in this situation. The spleen chakra is the Indian svadhisthana chakra and is a transportation system for energy in the body (Nest, 2018). It does not have anything in common with the spleen organ, however, but the spleen's function of purifying blood may be related to the spleen chakra's function of purifying energy.

An open sacral chakra demonstrates open and appropriate expression of emotions, comfortability regarding sexuality, and no problem handling matters of intimacy. Overly stoic people who tend to be unemotional or constantly apathetic and hard to reach typically have an underperforming sacral chakra. An overactive sacral chakra can, on the other hand, cause a person to be overly sexual, emotional, very clingy, and attach themselves to people in an unhealthy, often self-destructive way. The sacral chakra is thrown off balance when guilt becomes overwhelming. This imbalance steals a person's sense of having a right to feel, often worsening the very cause of the problem in a vicious self-sustaining cycle.

Perception of the senses is heavily associated with the sacral chakra. Smell, touch, sight, sound, and taste are all enhanced when the sacral chakra is open and balanced. While the root chakra is all about stability and foundation, the sacral chakra is like water in its flow. This chakra opens up into the realm of fluidity, movement, expression, and emotions (Hurst, 2017). The sacral chakra places an emphasis on forming an identity, and some reflection of who you are as a person is key. With this newfound understanding of your own identity also comes a greater understanding of others, and a stronger ability to form compassionate, harmonious relationships. It is especially important to remember when working on your sacral chakra to avoid becoming excessively dependent on others. You must feel able to depend on yourself. Continue to build off of that self-dependency while also growing your connections with others – this will actually result in far healthier, more enjoyable relationships than if you were to be highly dependent or uncertain of yourself.

The sacral chakra is all about emotions, and a closed off sacral chakra can indicate one of two extremes: an excitedly over-emotional person, or a stoic, numb, detached person. Depression is not uncommon in these cases, along with panic attacks and anxiety. In addition to these psychological responses, several physical ailments are also connected to a closed or otherwise off-balance sacral chakra. Low blood sugar or hypoglycemia, fatigue, lower back pain, spleen and kidney complications, and irregular menstrual cycles in women.

Building up from the prior chakra's connection through the feet and "roots," the sacral chakra benefits from dance and rhythmic movements. Activities such as Zumba, ballet, tap, and other forms of dance – even if that for you simply means jumping around in your bedroom to a song on the radio – help open the sacral chakra. Any exercise or activity involving a movement of the hips is also good for your sacral chakra's energy flow, making dance and Zumba excellent candidates, along with hula-hooping and hip raises.

Your inner artist is directly connected to the sacral chakra, and this cannot be ignored. Returning to buried artistic passions is one way to get back in touch with a creative outlet and repair the sacral chakra. Playing an instrument you used to love, painting, drawing, acting, sculpting, writing, journaling or art journaling, sewing, creating found poetry, crocheting, wood cutting or carving, and photography are all good examples of arts you may have engaged in a while back and should consider trying to return to for a little while. Sometimes artists will abandon their craft in the heat of life's constant pressures and demands, and once they pick it back up they are surprised and just how incomplete and awful they felt – without ever even being totally aware of it – without that self-expression. You don't have to paint the next Mona Lisa to accomplish the goal here. You just need to discover a way for you to express yourself. Self-expression not only relieves stress and potentially creates beautiful works of art made with your own hands, it only gives you a positive coping tool to use in managing your emotions, the key to opening your sacral chakra.

Exercises for Sacral Chakra

There are several exercises that can help you with this chakra. One is an exercise that you have already done. Breathing and moving the abdominal area in rhythm will help this chakra. Pelvic thrusts are also the best movements to help open this chakra. These will help to free up the chakra and in turn, help you to heal.

Foods and Drinks for Sacral Chakra

The color related to the sacral chakra can also be your basis for selecting foods for the second energy center. As orange is the corresponding color for the second chakra, your best options include oranges, papaya, peach and apricot. You may also consume carrots to enhance both your sacral and root chakras. Don't forget pumpkins.

Because of its association with the water element, drinking water, teas and broths is helpful in balancing the sacral chakra. You may also consume shrimp, crab, lobster, fish and other types of seafood. Fruit juices are ideal for the sacral chakra as well. Coconut, watermelon and mangoes are your best sources.

Aside from fruit slices, munch on almonds and walnuts for your snack time. To make meals and beverages for sacral chakra more flavorful, add vanilla, cinnamon, carob, caraway seeds, sesame seeds, and sweet paprika.

Associated Crystals

Carnelian, Chrysoprase, Sunstone

Carnelian stabilizes, grounds and anchors the energy into one's present reality. It removes the fear of death and enhances acceptance of the cycle of life. It has the capacity to cleanse other crystals. It helps to overcome negative conditioning and promotes self-trust. It calms anger and discards emotional negativity.

Benefits

It stimulates the sacral chakra and increases fertility. It simulates the metabolism. It heals lower back pain arthritis, rheumatism, depression and neuralgia. It improves the blood supply to the organs. It regulates the kidneys and body fluids and accelerates healing. It improves the body's absorption of vitamins and minerals.

Placement

You may place it in close contact with the skin. You may wear it as a pendant or belt buckle. When placed near the front door of your home, it invites abundance into your home and also invokes protection.

Protection

It protects against resentment, rage and envy. It promotes positive life choices, dissipates apathy and encourages a successful business. It helps to overcome abuse. It disperses mental lethargy.

Source

Peru, Iceland, Romania, India, Britain, Czech Republic,

Slovakia.

Chrysoprase energizes the sacral chakra and brings energy into the body. It enhances meditation and personal insight. It stimulates creativity. It aligns one's ideals with their behavior. It promotes positivity and brings about a sense of security and trust. It supports independence and promotes dexterity and fluency of speech.

Benefits

It treats heart problems, skin disease, and goiters and balances the hormones. It can be used as an aid for gout, eye problems and mental illness. It soothes the digestive system and as an elixir, it also calms stomach problems. It enhances the body's ability to absorb vitamin C. It enhances fertility and reverses infertility caused by infection.

Placement

It is very effective as an elixir (in severe cases). You may wear or place it as appropriate.

Protection

It helps to overcome impulsive or compulsive thoughts and behavior. It opposes feelings of judgment and promotes forgiveness and compassion. It disperses recurrent images and prevents nightmares (especially in children).

Source

Brazil, Russia, Tanzania, United States, Australia, Poland.

Sunstone it clears all the chakras and brings light and energy into the body. It is linked to good luck and fortune. It enhances the connection to light and the regenerative powers of the sun. It heightens intuition. It promotes vitality, independence, self-empowerment, confidence and feelings of self-worth. It aids in the elimination of heavy and suppressed emotions.

Benefits

It helps in nurturing oneself. It harmonizes the organs and regulates the autonomic nervous system. It alleviates depression. It relieves aches and pains, rheumatism and cartilage problems. It aids a sore throat and also relieves stomach ulcers.

Placement

It is beneficial to use it in the sun. You may hold, place or wear as feels appropriate.

Protection

It helps to "cut ties" with other people. It is also effective in removing emotional or mental "hooks" from other people, and the sunstone lovingly returns this energy to the other person. Keep it with you if you have a tendency of never saying "no" to other people. It reverses feelings of failure.

Source

Greece, United States, India, Norway, Canada.

Meditation Pose

Deviasana (the goddess pose)

- Assume a standing position with your feet very wide apart.
- Your toes should be pointed outwards.
- Drop your hips so that both of your knees are in perfect line with each of your ankles.
- Your hands must be situated on your thighs in a relaxed position.
- Pull your coccyx downwards.
- Take deep breaths.

- Perform side to side movement. As you do this, make sure that you sway your pelvis back and forth. This motion draws focus towards your organs of reproduction.

- While doing this, envision the color orange lighting your sacral chakra.

- Chant the word "Yam".

- Maintain this position for a minimum of eight breaths and a maximum of ten breaths.

Whenever you perform this pose, you are affecting the area of your life which governs fertility. It's not just about sexuality and reproduction but also about your ability to create things.

Chapter 7: Base/Root Chakra

It is also known as the muladhara chakra (Freshwater, 2017). The primal, basic needs come first and all of the others are built off of its satisfaction. Shelter, food, water, and safety make up the needs of this energy center. The root chakra related to these needs is located at the base of the spine, around the first three vertebrae, the tailbone area or pelvic floor.

This chakra is accountable for the sense of security, survival instincts, sense of being "there," sense of home, and grounding. A balanced root chakra should make you feel secure and stable, your space should feel like it is enough to satisfy you. An unbalanced root chakra might make you feel paranoid, often afraid or anxious, defensive, aggressive, restless, or overly self-conscious. Imbalances in the root chakra occur with fear and validate a person's sense of a right to exist, either in general, in a specific person's presence or in a particular place. They are also often connected to eating disorders. An overactive root chakra tends to make a person very stubborn to change in efforts to retain a strong grasp on security.

Those in poverty or tight financial situations, where basic needs are not easily or consistently met, are the most susceptible to an upset root chakra. If stable housing, figuring out which bills will and will not get paid this month, affording to eat, or paying the rent are a concern, chances are the root chakra is suffering. This also applies if you are struggling with an eating disorder, having food withheld from you, or are having fears of being kicked out of your home. Feelings of insecurity, paranoia, or constantly being on alert and feeling unsafe are not uncommon.

In order to heal the root chakra, you do not need to first resolve all immediate or temporary problems such as those listed above. If the root chakra is unbalanced, it isn't just because of bills being overdue recently or a fridge being empty for the time being – the connection is almost always deeper, buried within your psyche and constantly lingering. By inviting supportive energy into yourself, the root chakra can be refurbished and you will have a stronger foundation on which to build yourself. As this chakra is healed, what you need to survive, overcome constant fears, and feel safe will become more apparent.

The healthier your environment, the easier root chakra healing will be. If your home life, work environment, or overall neighborhood is negative, your root chakra will have a harder time remaining charged and open. If you are currently in a negative environment, consider ways you can change that environment for the better. What about your environment makes you feel the way you do? Do you feel safe at home, work, school, walking down the street, etc.? If you do come to the realization you are not living in a positive environment, try to create a small "safe space" for yourself. This space might include incense you find calming, good locks on the doors, and comfort items such as pillows or something to distract your attention and decrease anxiety. Design the space to be as comforting and secure for you as possible. Use this space as an anchor point where you can ground yourself. It is usually best if you are the only person who enters this space, as you want this particular area to feel as much like a personal sanctuary as possible. Beyond that, a plan should be considered for eventually leaving your environment if you cannot change the cause of your discomfort or fear. Alternatively, consider reaching out to someone you trust – such as a friend, relative, counselor, teacher, coach, or religious leader – about any situation that makes you feel uneasy or unsafe.

The root chakra is connected very closely with earth, and so getting in touch with nature will help in healing this chakra. Walking through the park, gardening, or even just purchasing and tending to a house plant are all ways to begin to get closer to earth and to nurture your root chakra. If you do not have a yard to garden in or an opportunity to interact with nature nearby, there are alternative options in addition to keeping an indoor plant that can help bring you closer to nature in your daily life. You may be able to seek out community gardens in your local area or offer to help an elderly person who needs a neighbor to help with their yard work. Planting seeds, feeling your feet or hands in the dirt, being around trees and growing life, and otherwise encountering nature are not only good for your psyche and root chakra, they are also known to directly nurture the soul.

Another method of connecting to the earth (without dirtying your hands or having to go past your bedroom) is visualization. Imagine deep roots made of either red or yellow light connecting to your root chakra, growing up from the center of the earth and uniting your chakra with the earth's core.

Feeling how alive you are and how your body works also aids in the healing process. The root chakra deals with matters of survival, stability, and basic needs. As such, it is a very physical chakra and thrives when you are moving your body in any way. Movement involving your legs and feet is especially helpful, such as taking a walk, dancing, doing lunges, stretching out your legs, or even just tapping your foot.

Perhaps the most challenging part of healing and charging the root chakra, for many people, is nurturing the quality our own self-reliance. If you don't feel capable of surviving or doing the things you need to do, it's hard to establish stability in your life. You are your own foundation, you must be reliable, strong, and resourceful for yourself, without leaning entirely on other people to take care of you. A line must be drawn between appropriately asking for help when it is needed and excessively depending on others. Reassure yourself that you are fine on your own, you are resourceful, and you are capable of getting what you need when you need it. Encouraging these perceptions of your own capabilities in a healthy way are key to healing and opening the root chakra. Having confidence in your ability to take care of yourself and ensure your basic needs are met is required when healing and opening the root chakra.

Open your mind to possibilities in your life. The root chakra thrives on stability, and part of stability actually includes knowledge of the option of fluidity. Many of us get hung up on things we view as final, concrete characteristics and traits. However, people are naturally far more fluid than given credit for. We can change our paths at any time, and taking opportunities outside of our established comfort zones is usually a very liberating, healthy thing to do. Especially when getting to know ourselves and our needs while opening the root chakra, it is important to know both who you are and acknowledge the life you live now and to understand that you can always cultivate a better life and make positive changes. This process will most likely include questioning your beliefs about what is important and what abundance and success mean to you personally.

Taking a count of your blessings and where you thrive and can thrive will, in turn, feed your root chakra's energy. For some of us, it's incredibly hard to think of anything all that good about what's going on in life at the present moment. Financial situations, poor health, personal and relationship struggles, death and bereavement, internal conflicts, natural disasters, and other negative events and scenarios can make the entire world seem a little too dim to cope with. When nurturing the root chakra, it can be helpful to take all of your blessings into account and recognize where you are abundant and fortunate, even if you are lacking in other areas. Not everyone has the same blessings, and that's okay. You don't have to be extremely prosperous in every aspect of life in order to appreciate what you do have. Consider loved ones, friends, pets, kind and generous people you run into throughout the day, the things you love most about the people around you, nature, health, access to food or water, luxuries and comforts, things and hobbies you enjoy, your job, and anything else you can think of. If you feel like it and would benefit from the visual, make a list of everything and everyone you are grateful for. Keep that list somewhere safe and look at it when you feel you need a reminder, occasionally adding to it if you become aware of more areas of your life in which you are actually quite rich. If you struggle to think of anything to write down, consider asking a good friend to help you with this list.

Potential Causes of Interference with the Root Chakra

If someone says that they are trying to fix a troubled root chakra they usually means that they are attempting to open up constricted pathways of energy that are causing deficiency. But in some cases, the pathways aren't blocked, but rather, they are simply overused. The first step of fixing an imbalanced root chakra is to ascertain whether the chakra is deficient or overactive. Fortunately for us, there are some pretty easy to follow cues that aid in this determination.

If a person is excessively sluggish, for example, with a distinct lack of energy, that person is most likely suffering from a deficient chakra. If on the other hand, someone is hyper, constantly in a state of agitation, and excessively vigilant, they just might have an overactive chakra. Those with an overactive chakra will also exhibit traits such as flashes of anger, excessive round-the-clock work, and even instances of hoarding. In the end, all of this behavior is due to a deep sense of insecurity.

Here are some direct causes of interference with the root chakra:

- Being Disorganized

There is an expression: "A disorganized home is the cause of a disorganized mind." You can also say that a disorganized home is the cause of a disorganized root chakra! Because it's very true that having a disorganized living space, work place, or even just a disordered weekly schedule can have direct impact upon your root chakra. As you can see, if you would like to restore your root chakra, cleaning your house might actually be a good start. But this effort of organization is more than straightening up your home and office – it also comes down to straightening up your goals and priorities in life. If you feel like you are becoming disconnected from your root chakra you just might want to do a self-evaluation, and figure out exactly what is important to you in life, and how you can work toward pursuing those goals.

- Becoming Alienated

It may seem like a bit of a redundancy, but if you are feeling the alienating symptoms of a busted root chakra, it just might be because you have become alienated. You see, some forms of alienation are not always within our control and can catch us off guard, breaking through all of our defenses. Environmental factors often come into play with this. If someone is in a situation or environment in which they constantly feel at odds with those around them, this can lead to significant damage to their root chakra. Ultimately, feelings of alienation stem from feeling unaccepted by either your immediate friends and family or society at large. One needs to take a proactive stance of unity and love in order to prevent such an experience. If you feel that you are indeed becoming alienated from your peers or society at large, you should find ways to participate in social gatherings. Whether you join a church, a volunteer group, or a social club, make sure that you find a way to put yourself around a group of good people to become connected with.

- Money Trouble

In modern human society, money is inescapably interwoven with our security and sense of well-being. It is, therefore, not surprising that trouble with finances can lead to the insecurity felt by a disrupted root chakra. Interestingly enough, the converse is true as well, and it could be a lack of self-worth and "rootedness" that can cause issues with money in the first place. Either way, money trouble can most certainly be attributed to a faulty root chakra. When the energy is not flowing through your root chakra the right way, it could lead to disruptions in your checkbook through bad financial decisions. So, if finances are giving you grief, you just might want to get to the root of the issue by taking a look at the state of your root chakra.

- Chronic Illness

In some cases, chronic physical ailments, especially those connected to the immune system, can cause the development of blockages in your root chakra. In such instances, the person is slowly worn down by a very real threat to their physical condition. And since the root chakra is our sense of stability in the physical world, it is only natural for it to begin to waver and shut down, just as the physical body begins to do so. If this chakra is disrupted, chronic illness could be a result.

- Troubled Relationships

Being in troubled personal relationships can, after a time, take a toll on your root chakra and have you questioning your core beliefs, doubting who you even are. If no other reason can be ascertained as to why a root chakra is blocked, troubled relationships could be a contributing factor. Sometimes, you just need to make an evaluation of those around you and try to determine just what it is you are getting out of the relationship.

Symptoms of a Blocked Root Chakra

According to tradition, it is when this root chakra is compromised by constant states of fear, dread, and anxiety that we end up having a significant disruption in the "flow of our lifeforce". This can cause a very real problem when it comes to our interpersonal relationships, and daily functionality in life. Since someone with a blocked root chakra feels quite literally "uprooted", they may feel out of place—that they literally "don't belong on this Earth".

Signs of a blocked root chakra:

- A Preoccupation with Material Wealth

Those with a blocked root chakra often have an unhealthy preoccupation with gaining material wealth. This obsession is actually rooted in the fear that the person has of losing their financial sustenance. It is out of this fear that people begin to greedily seek to acquire and hoard material wealth. They want to stock up as much as they can in case they ever have to do without. Such an unbalanced sentiment is certainly not healthy for your root chakra. Those with such a disruption to their chakra will begin to become greedy with their material goods and at the most extreme end of it, they just might become hoarders.

- Deep Distrust of Those Around You

When someone does not have a rooted chakra, they can face severe disruptions in their ability to trust others. The doubt that they feel about their place in the world and how they should interact with those around them is so great that they end up becoming paralyzed by it. In order for your root chakra to remain open, it doesn't mean you have to be naïve, but you have to at least be open to the possibility of trust. Failure to develop a rudimentary level of trust leads to a direct blockage of your root chakra.

- All Work and No Play

Many might contend that being a so-called "workaholic" is a good thing, but in many cases, it is the sign of a major disruption in a person's core values. When someone cannot balance their work and personal life, sooner or later they are going to experience some issues. And often enough, this imbalance begins with a blocked root chakra. You don't want to be the person who prefers to work the late shift at the hospital rather than spending Christmas with their family. Even though work is generally a positive thing, having priorities skewed in such a fashion is simply not healthy. So, as important as down time is, it is wise to always make room for some of it.

- Dysfunctional Family

If someone's core self is disrupted by a blockage of their root chakra, this can then translate into all of their other aspects of their family life. Ripples of discord will inevitably reach those closest to them, often leading to family dysfunction. Simply put—if one member of the family isn't feeling right, then neither is anyone else. Such things are a major sign of a blocked root chakra.

- Hypervigilance

When someone is experiencing episodes of hypervigilance, they are in a constant state of alert—constantly standing vigil for any perceived threat in their environment. This state of hypervigilance could be a good thing in certain situations, such as for soldiers in a warzone or for a hunter in a lion-infested jungle, but for most of us, most of the time, this state of hyper-alertness is just not beneficial. For someone sitting at their desk inside a cubicle in a bustling office space for example, the fact that they can't stop hearing and vigilantly focusing on every single sound around them only leads to severe distraction from their work. This inability to tune out the environment can then eventually lead to severe cases of anxiety. It is no coincidence that the above-mentioned example of the soldier in the warzone often has an acute case of PTSD upon returning to normal conditions. It is due to the fact that they developed a state of hypervigilance while deployed, and are unable to bring their senses back to baseline upon their return. In all of these cases, their root chakra has been completely blocked off, and they are stuck in a constant feedback loop of hypervigilant alertness without cause. In order to get things back to normal, the root chakra needs to be opened back up once again. Being constantly hypervigilant and on edge is not an easy way to live life, and needs to be corrected.

- Chronic Anxiety

As mentioned in the previous section, anxiety and a blocked root chakra go hand in hand. When there is a disruption of the flow of energy in this important circuit of the body, sense of self, purpose, and control become lost, leading to feelings of anxiety and unease. If you are suffering from chronic anxiety it could be a sign of a blocked root chakra. You will learn how to work toward correcting this condition a little further on in this chapter.

- Hard to Be Yourself

This one is actually a dead giveaway when it comes to a malfunctioning muladhara —because if you have difficulty being your true self around others, it is pretty clear evidence that your core self has been disrupted. Your roots are who you are. It is the essential personality you were born with. If you are not being yourself, your root chakra has been compromised. If this is the case, you need to reexamine your trajectory in life and perhaps make an abrupt change of course in order to get back on track and get back to your roots.

- Eating Disorder

These kinds of disorders are rampant in modern society, and there is the potential of a blocked root chakra manifesting itself in the form of an eating disorder. This is due to the fact that the need for food is directly connected to our need to feel love. Often enough, if someone has a negative self-image this can then translate into developing an eating disorder. The individual feels unaccepted, and unworthy of love, so they in turn feel unworthy of food, leading to starvation diets or bouts of binge and purge eating. An eating disorder is a clear sign of a malfunctioning root chakra and needs to be addressed immediately.

Exercises for Root Chakra

The exercises needed to help you with this chakra are easy to do. Take off your shoes and socks and get ready to stamp your feet on the ground. As you do so, be aware that the whole foot should touch the ground. This is the chakra that relates to that feeling of being grounded. The exercises should be performed several times over a five minute period before relaxing with your feet flat on the floor. You will also find a guide to the foods that you should be eating in the next section of the book. If you take yoga classes, ask your teacher to introduce you to the bridge pose as this is particularly good for the root chakra. This is where your body is supported by the balls of your feet and your flat hands. You may need supervision the first time that you try this, or you can try using a video, which will provide an idea of how the exercise should be properly performed.

Remember that the root chakra is important for helping you to feel grounded in the world. You will want to make sure that you are able to feel like you belong in the physical world, without feeling so attached to it that you forget all that is going on around you. It is not a good idea to focus too much on the material things in your life, as they are going to leave you feeling lost and confused because the chakra is going to start failing.

This is why spending some time out in nature and just feeling the earth beneath your feet is so important for helping you to feel great and full. You will be able to touch the earth and learn what really matters, while hopefully being able to release some of the materialistic things that are going on in the world around you. Try to save a few minutes each week at least, although doing it each day is the best option, and just work on being outside, touching the grass, and even walking around in your backyard to help make the root chakra feel better.

Foods and Drinks for Root Chakra

Being associated with the earth element and the virtue of being grounded, the best foods for your root chakra are those dug or derived from the ground. These include potatoes, yams, beets, rutabagas, turnips, parsnips, ginger and garlic.

Eggs, meat, soy products and other protein-rich foods are beneficial for the root chakra, as well. As for spices, you can try meals seasoned with cayenne, chives, hot paprika and black pepper.

But generally, any produce will benefit the first chakra. After all, fruits and vegetables are derived from the earth which is the element associated with root chakra.

Reddish fruits and vegetables are also ideal for the root chakra. Among these are apples, strawberries and pomegranates.

Roasting potatoes, yams and other root vegetables is an ideal way of preparing food for your root chakra. The fire element can enhance the ability of the root chakra. You may opt to season some of them with salt and olive oil to make them more palatable.

Associated Crystals

Black Tourmaline, Fire Agate, Garnet, Hematite, Red Jasper

Black Tourmaline grounds the energy. It disperses stress and tension and increases physical vitality. It clears negative thoughts and encourages a positive attitude. It stimulates creativity and selflessness. In healing, when placed point-out from the body, it draws off negative energy.

Benefits

It strengthens the immune system, it relieves pain, it treats arthritis and learning disorders, and it defends against debilitating diseases and helps realign the spinal column.

Placement

You may wear it around your neck or place it between yourself and the source of electromagnetics.

Protection

It protects against cell phones, negative energies, any ill wishes, radiation, electromagnetic smog, and psychic attacks.

Source

Brazil, United States, Italy, Sri Lanka, Africa, Afghanistan and Western Australia.

Fire Agate grounds the energy and stimulates vitality on all levels. It is supportive during difficult times. As its name suggests, it is linked to the fire element, thus it aids in sexual endeavors. It can be beneficial in treating addictions. It encourages introspection, aids relaxation, instills spiritual strength and enhances meditation.

Benefits

It brings vitality into the body. It heals the stomach, circulatory disorders, and the endocrine and nervous systems. It can reduce hot flashes and remove heat from the body. It supports the eyes, enhances night vision and clears one's inner vision at an intuitive level. It clears etheric blockages and has an energizing effect on the aura.

Placement

You may wear fire agate for long period of time. You may also place it appropriately on the head or the body.

Protection

As it is very calming, it brings safety and security. It is a very protective crystal, which protects against all ill wishes and builds a protective shield around the body. It sends harm back to the source.

Source

Morocco, Brazil, United States, Czech Republic, India, Iceland.

Garnet cleanses and energizes the chakras. It purifies, balances and revitalizes the energy. It alleviates emotional tension, it balances the sex drive and inspires love, devotion and commitment. It brings hope to seemingly hopeless situations and it is helpful in traumatic situations.

Benefits

It stimulates the metabolism, it purifies and reenergizes the blood, heart and lungs. It regenerates the body and DNA. It assists in the absorption of vitamins and minerals and it treats cellular and spinal disorders.

Placement

You may wear this in close contact with the skin, such as on the fingers, over the heart or on the earlobes. Place it on the brow chakra (third eye) for past-life regression.

Protection

It clears negative chakra energy. It dissolves old behavior patterns (which no longer serve you well), it helps to release old and obsolete ideas. It removes inhibitions and circumvents unconscious, self-induced sabotage. It brings success in business.

Source

Worldwide.

Hematite grounds and protects the energy. It balances the meridians, it dissolves negative energy and also prevents negative energy from entering the aura. It harmonizes the body, mind and spirit, by restoring peace.

Benefits

It assists in overcoming addictions and compulsions. It can draw heat from the body. It treats overeating, smoking, any form of overindulgence and helps to accept past mistakes. It enhances memory, stimulates concentration and focus. It restores, regulates and strengthens the blood supply.

Placement

You may place or hold this appropriately for calming and healing. To facilitate in spinal manipulation, place it at the top and base of the spine. Hematite should not be used for long periods of time, or in areas where inflammation is present.

Protection

It is beneficial in legal situations. It supports nervous people and enhances their ability to survive, it enhances reliability, will power and boosts self-esteem.

Source

Switzerland, Italy, Britain, Brazil, Canada, Sweden.

Red Jasper grounds and protects the energy and aligns the chakras. It balances the yin and yang and aligns the physical, mental and emotional bodies with the etheric realm. It facilitates in dream recall and shamanic journeys. It is supportive during stressful times and reminds people to help one another.

Benefits

It detoxifies and strengthens the blood, the liver and the circulatory system. It dissolves blockages in the liver and bile ducts. It enhances courage to deal with problems. It promotes quick thinking. It merges all aspects of one's life into one. It stimulates the imagination helps one to transform ideas into action. It is supportive during illness or hospitalization.

Placement

As it works slowly, you may use it for long periods of time. It may be in close contact with the skin. A large jasper in a room will absorb negative energy. You may place it at the root chakra or as appropriate. You may also place it underneath your pillow.

Protection

It absorbs negative energy and cleanses the chakras and aura. It clears environmental and electromagnetic pollution, as well as radiation. When played with as a "worry bead", it has a very calming effect on the emotions.

Source

Worldwide.

Meditation Pose

Vrksasana (the tree pose)

- Assume a standing position. Make sure that your feet are apart so that you are able to achieve a steady balance.
- While performing an outbreath, relax your knees. Drop your coccyx while you engage your thighs.
- Then bring up your right foot towards the inner part of your left thigh so that you are standing only on your left foot. If you are unable to do this, place the sole of your right foot against your left inner calf instead.
- Breathe deeply in a relaxed manner.
- Let gravity ground you. Feel the life-giving energy moving up your spine.
- Imagine the color red illuminating in your root chakra.
- While doing this, chant the word "Lam".
- Maintain this position for five breaths. Then, you may switch sides.

Whenever you practice this position, you are affecting the area in your life which governs familial relations and feelings of self-preservation. This pose provides you with confidence so that you will be able to stand up by yourself.

Conclusion

I hope this book was able to help you develop your awareness of the principal chakras and what each one signifies. By knowing, you have by now learned which ones to call upon when you need a little extra help, whether it is a need to keep you grounded to your relationships around you (root), or to enhance your love life (sacral), or to boost your self-confidence (solar plexus). If not, to experience ultimate balance, peace, wellness and harmony (heart), or to express yourself clearly (throat), or to be profound with your vision and intuition (third eye), or to gain knowledge and enlightenment (crown).

By now, you are ready to practice basic chakra meditation for healing, balancing and feeling energized and recharged. You now have a comprehensive understanding of working with your chakras, such as being aware of your blocked chakras and the various ways you can work to clear them, vitalizing your energy and visualizing your healing process. After all, guiding and helping you in your pursuit of wellness and wholeness of your being is the primary sole purpose of this book.

You will soon be able to discover there is no limit as to how the chakras can help you be the best you can be. You will feel as though life is going the way you want it to, and if ever problems crop up, you will take them in stride. Everything good falls into place within you, including a holistic healing physically, emotionally, mentally and spiritually. Now, you can consider adding greater depth to your chakric journey by exploring intermediate and advanced methods of working with your chakras, including reiki.

Therefore, make yourself a promise to set aside ten minutes a day to get your energies flowing and you will see just how good you can feel. Although it may seem a little overwhelming at first, with regular practice, you will soon find that the exercises come naturally to you and the benefits appear almost immediately. You will feel at peace with yourself and happy, both with the person you are and the person you will become.

Thank you, and enjoy the journey!

References

Brief history of chakras. (n.d.). Della Luce. Retrieved from https://colourmedblog.wordpress.com/brief-history-of-chakras/

Freshwater, S. (2017). 1st chakra root muladhara. Shawna Freshwater, PhD. Retrieved from https://spacioustherapy.com/1st-chakra-root-muladhara/

Houston, D. (2019). Throat chakra: Meaning, properties and powers - the complete guide. CrystalsandJewelry.com. Retrieved from https://meanings.crystalsandjewelry.com/throat-chakra/

Hurst, K. (2017). Sacral chakra healing for beginners: How to open your sacral chakra. The Law Of Attraction. Retrieved from http://www.thelawofattraction.com/sacral-chakra-healing/

Judith, A. (n.d.). The history of the chakra system. Sequoiarecords.com. Retrieved from http://www.sequoiarecords.com/article-history-of-chakras/The+History+of+the+Chakra+System.html

Know your heart chakra and how to unlock its power. (2018). Chakras.info. Retrieved from https://www.chakras.info/heart-chakra/

Know your throat chakra and how to unlock its power. (n.d.). Chakras.info. Retrieved from https://www.chakras.info/throat-chakra/

Luna, A. (2017). The ultimate guide to third eye chakra healing for complete beginners. LonerWolf. Retrieved from https://lonerwolf.com/third-eye-chakra-healing/

Ness, K. (2018). Sacral chakra: Here's everything you need to know about your second chakra. YogiApproved™. Retrieved from https://www.yogiapproved.com/om/the-second-chakra-how-it-impacts-your-relationships-and-creativity/

Olesen, J. (2014). Crown chakra - the seventh chakra. Color-Meanings.com. Retrieved from https://www.color-meanings.com/crown-chakra-the-seventh-chakra/

Olesen, J. (2014). Throat chakra - the fifth chakra. Color-Meanings.com. Retrieved from https://www.color-meanings.com/throat-chakra-the-fifth-chakra/

The third eye chakra. (n.d.). Chakras.info. Retrieved from https://www.chakras.info/third-eye-chakra/

Things you should know about the solar plexus chakra. (2018). Mindmonia. Retrieved from https://mindmonia.com/solar-plexus-chakra/

REIKI FOR BEGINNERS

UNLOCKING THE SECRETS OF REIKI: A STEP-BY-STEP GUIDE TO REIKI HEALING FOR BEGINNERS TO ACHIEVE PHYSICAL AND SPIRITUAL WELLNESS

Caroline Kirkman

Introduction

Healing!

The word sums up the desires of many people in the world right now. Most people who want healing from something they are dealing with internally. However, the real question is, how can they get a long-term effect? It drives us to seek sustainable solutions, and at the top of the list, we have the answer: Reiki.

The Reiki story is unique. It speaks of a Japanese healing technique that aids in stress reduction and relaxation. It's generally administered by the laying of hands on the aching body part, supported by the concept of an unseen energy that flows within us.

People believe that if our life force is low, we become susceptible to illnesses or stress. When it is high, we can live a happy and healthy life. Reiki has helped many individuals with self-healing, but one of the fascinating aspects of this technique is that you can utilize it for distant healing. The practice entails sending energy across time and space to heal someone.

There is also a relationship between Reiki and chakras. Chakras are based on the concept of Yogi philosophy. They are like vortexes that aid the radiation of energy that corresponds with the physical body. Despite the presence of several chakras, the focus is always on the seven main ones as they emit light energy.

The purpose of Reiki is to heal and protect a person's body by striking a balance between their physical, mental, social, and emotional states. However, if a chakra is damaged or blocked, it will be unable to channel the energy in the right way. So, when they are balanced, they aid the successful transmission of the Reiki technique.

Nevertheless, this book isn't focused on chakras. Despite the connection between the two amazing methods, we will concentrate on Reiki and how you can use it to attain a good spiritual and physical well-being. For a more detailed insight into the relationship between the said techniques, you can get my book called *Chakras for Beginners, Healing Yourself With Chakras and Meditation. A Complete Guide to Third Eye and Chakra Healing for Starters With Practical Exercises to Balance Your Chakras.*

We are going to take on a journey towards healing profoundly and effectively. We will make several stops that will make up the entirety of the ideas from sections on how you can learn the practice of Reiki to the kind of ailments you may cure with this treatment. What you have in your hands is a complete Reiki guide that has been carefully put together to help you attain healing and more.

Are you ready to embark on this journey now? We will start with building a solid foundation on this topic with a detailed chapter on the Reiki story.

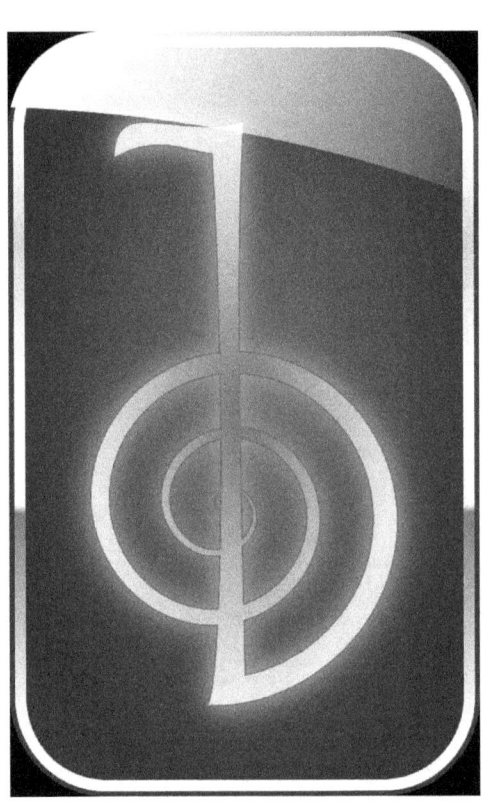

Chapter One: The Reiki Story

The first stop is a foundational one that entails complete details about the concept of Reiki. This chapter will provide insight into how the technique emerged, as well as the peculiarities of the process.

We'll cover a bit of the history of Reiki so that you can understand it better.

When you hear the word Reiki, you are listening to a combination of two Japanese words "Rei" and "Ki." Rei means a higher intelligence, God's wisdom, or higher power, while Ki refers to a spiritually guided life or non-physical energy that animates all living things.

The Reiki method of healing was established on the understanding of the body's energy system with a keen focus to restore balance. It was often used in self-care and offered in private practice and hospitals as a source of support therapy. It could be seen as a source of supportive therapy.

The form of Reiki practiced today has been in existence for over a hundred years. It began with Dr. Maiko Usui, the creator of the technique.

In modern usage of Reiki, you will discover a blend of medicine and psychology as these were the interests that drove Dr. Usui to seek ways to heal himself and others by the laying of hands. He wanted this practice to be accessible to everyone who needed healing.

So, how did Reiki become a global phenomenon from being a discovery that's made by one man?

After Dr. Usui's death, another doctor he had trained, Dr. Hayashi, took over in Tokyo and developed Reiki further by including the hand positions that could cover the body thoroughly. Dr. Hayashi also trained other Reiki maestros.

One of the Reiki masters, Mrs. Hawayo Takata, is a Japenese-American who got credited for bringing Reiki to the United States. Reiki saved Mrs. Takata from needing surgery. She enjoyed the process, found it helpful and relaxing, and gained more knowledge before bringing it to the states. Just like Dr. Hiyashi, Mrs. Takata also made some positive changes to the Reiki system. Before passing away, she trained 22 Reiki masters (International Association of Reiki Professionals, 2019).

The people who practice Reiki today use the methods that were developed by Dr. Usui. These practitioners can do that to heal themselves while enhancing their well-being. The modern Reiki masters can provide energy to other people through a gentle, light pressure using the Reiki hand position.

Since its inception, Reiki has been known to assist people who are dealing with diseases, pain, illnesses, and so on. You will learn more about the specific problems Reiki can solve in the fourth chapter.

Reiki is a non-physical healing energy that is guided by a higher intelligence or spiritually guided life force. Reiki is used to aid the body's natural healing abilities, reduce stress, and promote relaxation. This technique uses a hands-on approach as a way to transmit the unforeseen energy that flows from the practitioner to the patient.

Reiki is an intelligent energy that targets the area where healing is needed and restores harmony. Reiki practitioners assure that the treatment is bound to bring the required results as long as they follow the guides. They simply need to transmit life force into a recipient's body while focusing on key areas.

Today, many people have a backlog of physical issues they suppress. The reason is that they only concentrate on the surface of the problem, which is only a minute aspect of it. So, there are numerous ideas that become implemented to suppress the issue, which rises again occasionally because it hasn't been dealt with entirely.

With Reiki, the approach is different in a positive way. You get an opportunity to heal the source of the problem, not the symptoms. When you show up for a session, you should be ecstatic because you will get rid of your ailment once and for all.

If a person seeks out Reiki for a back issue, for example, the focus will not be on giving them relief but healing the source of the pain, thus removing the causes and effects of the problem entirely. Of course, the symptoms may not disappear immediately; however, with consistent Reiki sessions, healing will take place as time will prove to work on this.

Modern Reiki is gaining popularity just as the list of Reiki masters increases every day. People only become interested in becoming a master at something when they know it works for sure and that it will enable them to help others.

Reiki is also used in cancer clinics, spas, wellness centers, and hospitals. Some of them have a Reiki program in addition to other healing practices. Others stick with Reiki only because they are already convinced that it will yield the desired results.

Most professionals like to describe Reiki as a holistic healing system because it relates to the whole being and cuts across the physical, emotional, mental, and spiritual aspects of an individual. The body isn't viewed as a separate piece with different functions when doing Reiki. Instead, it is seen as a web of energy where everything works in agreement to provide balance for each part.

To attain good health, every aspect of the body has to be in tandem, and this is what Reiki tries to ensure. You need the continuous flow of life force to be healthy. Once there is an imbalance with this flow, you will start to experience negative emotions and health complications.

The masters of Reiki firmly believe that the universal energy is responsible for the bodily processes. This is the reason why every session will be about keeping that balance intact. Through the hands of the practitioner, the universal energy flows into the body of the receiver, which will aid in the healing procedure.

Reiki therapists often find clarity with their purpose in life because they notice that attending therapy consistently can boost their mindfulness through meditation, use of sacred symbols, precepts, and mantras that the practitioners can navigate through while performing hands-on healing.

Another fascinating thing about Reiki is that it doesn't cause any damage to the body. There is a lot of apprehension within individuals when they are offered a healing process that doesn't entail the use of drugs, surgery, or any other medical enabler. Their fears are real because no one wants to get hurt while trying to get healed, right? Well, if you are afraid of this practice, you should know that Reiki doesn't harm anyone who tries it.

Some Reiki masters say that they do not consider themselves as healers because they believe that the body is its own healer and that what they do is transmit the universal energy while the body does the rest of the work. Furthermore, they believe that the process of giving Reiki to someone else gives them more life energy. So, it is merely a case of giving extra power to do more and reawaken the positive vibes that make a person feel great about themselves again and enable healing.

We are swarmed by activities in the modern world; hence, we run around empty with just enough energy to go through what we can take for a day. This means that there is no more gas left for maintenance or more profound healing. When you offer your body universal energy, though, it uses this source for bodily repair.

If you are discovering Reiki now through this book, one thing you should know for sure is the fact that there are no limits to the possibilities it offers. If you look back at the brief history that we have just talked about, you will agree that the different changes and improvements made by each of the earliest Reiki masters indicate that the techniques and skills will always develop through time.

Reiki's energy comes from an infinite source. Even if the methods see innovation in the future, we will still be dealing with the same kind of energy that was used in the past. When a person meditates on Reiki's energy even when passing the treatment to others, they are aware of the positive essence that's embedded in the universal energy.

The latter goes beyond the state of consciousness and introduces the feeling of happiness, peace, and joy. These feelings are not just a figment of the imagination but a palpable experience that will help you achieve healing. People who have stayed true to the Reiki experience agree that as they get better, the practice not only helps them deal with their illnesses but also other issues.

In addition to healing from diseases, you will observe more positive traits with your personality when you start learning Reiki. However, in the beginning, you must identify your unhealthy features and become willing to let them go. After all, Reiki respects free will. When you accept the practice in your life, you must also surrender to its spiritual path, allow the process to heal you entirely, and develop the qualities that are healthy for you.

As your quality of life improve, you will notice that the more Reiki sessions you attend, the more deeply connected you become with your personality, emotions, and personal beliefs. All of them can contribute to your emotional well-being.

The first thing that you probably did after reading the title was to skimp through the Table of Contents because you wanted to find out what was in store for you in the actual chapters. Despite that, it is a good thing that you have taken a step towards learning by reading the actual content.

You may have read a sentence representing a chapter in the table, but here you are, reading more than three pages for that one sentence. Why? The reason is that the essence of greatness isn't defined by the introductory points. This idea is true for Reiki at least.

When you go to your first Reiki session, you may be looking forward to do some hands-on healing because that is what you have seen other masters do. However, you will also discover that there is so much to unearth about the process. You may even decide to go for a session because of physical or emotional pain that you have been dealing with silently and get healed from it.

So, I am not saying that Reiki is focused on one thing at a time, which makes it quite fascinating. Patience, non-competitiveness, self-love, and love for others are some of the positive, healthy traits you will start to develop after attending more profound sessions. If you have struggled with accepting others for who they are, you can also be sure that Reiki will help you move to a place of acceptance while gaining the power to forgive quickly.

Now, we will deliberate more on the benefits of Reiki in two other chapters, so we don't have to express such interests in detail here. With the use of Reiki comes the access to the energy flow it represents.

Have you ever gotten a library card before? If you had a library card, then you would know that it gives you access to all the books in the library. Still, it doesn't mean that you will read the entire collection of books that it houses.

Well, the same idea applies to Reiki. Through the first sessions you engage in, you will gain access to the universal energy. Will you get to channel the most effective qualities of Reiki, though? No. You have access to the energy just as you have done with your library card, so you need to utilize this privilege and build on the power that you have received by going for more sessions.

Like the situation with the library card, you may not be able to read all the books in there, but you can go through a large pile as long as you keep on going to the library and using the card. You will experience a higher level of peace, joy, and love during each session, which further opens you up to get healed through Reiki.

Regardless of what is written or said about Reiki, it is better to be experienced than heard. Like Mrs. Takata said, "I can't tell you, but I can show you."

Going forward from this chapter, you will only encounter practical ideas that will provide insight into the Reiki experience. The next section will give you details on how you can learn the practice, so enjoy reading!

Chapter Two: How to Learn Reiki

Welcome to the first chapter of the practical aspect of our journey. Now that you know the theoretical points of the subject matter, we will take you through a series of steps that you can utilize to learn how to practice Reiki.

As it was clearly stated in the previous chapter, there are higher levels of universal energy. We may not be able to take on all of them because it requires a lot of training, but what you will receive here is a solid foundation and a good start for your Reiki practice.

The system that you will be exposed to is the same one used by Dr. Mikao Usui. Through this system, you will experience amazing improvements in your personal, emotional, and spiritual well-being. You can also observe changes in the lives of the people you share this process with. Hence, it is a great way to introduce Reiki into your relationships.

The variants of Reiki have been used worldwide by holy men, healers, and Rishis. They used to believe that everything in the world was made up of vibrational energy. The system also works because it improves the energetic make-up of the body, which makes it possible for the root causes of the problem to be handled.

When you heal with Reiki, three things can happen to you:

1. Your body's energetic blueprints are improved.
2. Your body adopts the new state causing much healing.
3. You can tap into the universal energy flow.

The first step that you can take towards the mastery of Reiki is your choice to focus on the entirety of your system while inviting the grace to heal, clear all the mental barriers in your head, and believe in the efficacy of the steps that will be shared below.

Please remember that this is a practical chapter. You must read everything carefully because you can use them to apply Reiki healing into your life.

Steps for Learning Reiki

Step 1: Connect With the Universal Energy

Universal energy is the building block for reality, and it is everywhere. It explains the discovery made by scientists that the universal energy field genuinely exists all around us. Reiki healers tap into this energy pool and then channel it to provide life-changing benefits for us and their patients.

For you to tap into the universal energy, your consciousness needs to increase to a higher level where you can tune yourself into the realities that exist beyond the physical world — a realm of emotions, love, thoughts, and heightened spirituality.

Some people are always skeptical of this first step because they erroneously believe that they don't have the "gift" to form this secure connection with the energy source. Well, those Reiki masters who have access to the highest forms dedicated their lives to studying and practicing. If you have the diligence and determination to settle with each step and practice for a long time, you will surely have a success story to tell. But first, you must handle this initial stage before perfecting the others.

Step #1 entails that you must make a connection with the universal energy, which has a consciousness. To begin this process, you must clear your mind and ask for permission to be used as a healing channel first.

Speak the Reiki invocation out loud or think about it. The words have to be in line with your beliefs. You can say simple words, such as "I ask the power and wisdom of universal energy to allow me to become a channel for infinite love and healing…"

The invocation above is just an example. You can create yours, but the point is that you need to ask the universal energy for its help so that it can channel its gift to you. By acknowledging that you need assistance, you will be giving up any claim you may have had in the past to the power of your own.

Next, you need to visualize the energy entering your palms. Visualization is so powerful because it allows you to connect with the energy (you will observe as we make progress that visualization cuts across almost all the steps). There are numerous visualization processes that will help you connect with universal Energy, but you can utilize the one that's known as INFINITE LIGHT:

- Close your eyes and breathe in.
- Exhale and visualize the beams of white energy all around you.
- Feel the energy from its infinite field.
- Inhale and when you exhale this time focus on your palms while using your will to call on the light around you.
- Visualize the light entering your body and flowing into your palms.
- Feel your palms as they radiate energy.

The most critical part of this step isn't getting every aspect of it right but feeling the energy, and this is what a lot of people haven't got right. By practicing the concept of universal energy visualization, you will be able to feel and sense it all around you.

When you visualize the connection taking place, you will be focused on your will that makes the link happen and then your thoughts, willpower and everything else that comes in contact with this energy flow will cause the Reiki reality to take shape.

You have a grasp on how to get in touch with universal energy. The next step will teach you how to detect negative energy present in your body.

Step 2: Perform an Aura Scan

An aura is a form of universal energy that surrounds objects and living things, but you may be surprised to know that your body does not give off an aura because it is an overlay on it. To put it simply, you are not giving off an aura, but your aura is giving off you.

So, your aura puts off and absorbs information. It is a part of your energy system that can transmit and receive signals. Auras have different properties that cut across, sizes, patterns, textures, shapes, and colors.

All of your memories, emotions, thoughts, and experiences exist in your aura, and this plays a crucial role in affecting your health. Your body is a physical representation of your aura, and your physical health is also dependent on the health of your aura.

To explain the connection between your aura and your health, you've got to think back to when you harbored specific negative thoughts in your mind and how it affected you. In such moments, it starts to show up in your aura as a dark muddy clot, which then takes the shape of a physical symptom.

Whatever you feel is a manifestation of your aura. If you feel pain, are depressed, or have problems with your relationship, then it is safe to say they manifest from your aura. This feeling helps you realize what needs to be done to bring it back to a beneficial state enough to result in healing for the symptoms.

This second step requires you to be able to tell the areas of your aura that has problems and how you can sense the circumstances that led to the aura being the exact way it is now.

However, scanning your aura can be a worthless pursuit if you don't understand the life force optimization system, which is required to serve as a map for healing using high sensory perception and feelings with the hands.

When you become conscious of your aura, it will directly lead you to the next step of the process through which you can learn Reiki, and that step entails setting your healing intentions.

Step 3: Realize Your Healing Intention

This step and the previous ones will show you how to heal the underlying energetic problems that are responsible for the physical symptoms you experience.

Your healing intention is the result you would like to experience from the healing sessions. Do you remember going to the gym at any time, for instance? What were your expectations? Did you want better abs? A right waistline or a flat stomach?

The expectations you had when you registered for the gym helped to keep you accountable. This is the same with this third step. Regardless of what you want healing for, maybe an injury, a more positive emotional state or to find balance in your life, you must have healing expectations.

Your intention is your message!

When you send a message to your friend, you are communicating something to the person. However, with Reiki, the message is not received by the person who is going to be healed but by their aura.

If the message is clear and precise, the aura will accept it and transform it to match the positive message you are sending them. The aura then projects the new and improved state to the body.

You cannot have a Reiki session without an intention. Your healing plan tells the aura the form it should take. This means that before your session, you must spend time alone to discover what you seek healing from. Say, do you want to get over a trauma, improve your sleep, or overcome addiction?

The aura will only accept a dominant healing intention as this kind of intention can lead to a life-changing healing process that blossoms into reality, thus relieving you of the issues.

Again, with this step, you will have to rely on a Reiki process we introduced with the first step: visualization! With visualization, you can manifest your desires. Just imagine what your life would be like if you didn't have the challenge you are dealing with.

You should ask yourself what your life will be like without the pain and then try to visualize the answer. Imagine yourself healed and create vivid images in the mind of your healing intention coming to fruition.

If you want to use Reiki for back pain that has deprived you of dancing, for instance, don't go for the healing session focusing on the back pain. Instead, think about the kind of music you want to dance to once you are healed, visualize it, and take advantage of the positivity it brings.

Visualize the tissues in your back getting healed and the pain going away. This is how you set your healing intentions and work on rebuilding yourself to attain the healing you desire. Have you heard about Reiki symbols? Well, it is about time you discovered what they are and what you can do with them.

Step 4: Activate Reiki Symbols

Reiki symbols help you tune yourself to a particular level of frequencies that give you access to advanced abilities. The symbols have been used for generations, and they are fully imbibed with energy from great healers over the years.

In learning how to practice Reiki, you must choose the symbols you wish to utilize, and your decision is based on the abilities you desire to use. For example, you can use the mental and emotional symbol for issues relating to relationship challenges or an addiction.

So, what are the Reiki symbols?

The Power Symbol

This symbol can magnify healing energy and provide spiritual protection while empowering other symbols. The power symbol is known as *Cho Ku Rei*.

The Master Symbol

The Master symbol is the most potent symbol in Reiki that is used by the masters to heal a soul or treat illness and diseases in the body, thus creating a fantastic life change for the individual. The Master symbol is referred to as *Di KoMyo*.

The Distance Symbol

The Distance symbol is a unifying one that represents enlightenment and peace. The symbol is also used to send healing energy over distance and time to anyone who is in the past, present, or future. The Distance symbol is also known as *Hon Sha ZeShoNen*.

The Mental and Emotional Symbol

This symbol is tuned to the energies of love and well-being while being used for restoring calm to a person's mental and emotional states. The mental and emotional symbols can also be useful in removing addictions and releasing negative energies from a person. The Mental and Emotional symbol is also known as *Sei He Ki*.

Everything in the system and the steps you are following work harmoniously to transform your life through the universal energy. Regardless of where you are now or what your issues may be, you are dealing with the Reiki symbols that can be used to manifest the changes you seek.

What are you struggling with? Drugs, alcohol, emotional pain? All of these can change when you start allowing the universal energy into your life. Express gratitude while on this path, especially after activating the symbols mentioned above.

With these symbols, you can transmit healing energy into the areas of your body in need of a cure. Discover how to do this in the next step.

Step 5: Guide Healing Energy

Now, this fifth step is a culmination of all the other steps you read through up till this point. You may know that, as a healer, your hands can be positioned correctly to guide energy into the aura and chakras that need healing.

Despite that, the hand positions will not work by themselves. You need to manifest the healing by creating a secure connection with steps 1 to 4.

These steps, when used together, lay the foundation for your healing session and enable you to channel energy and use it for the right purpose. With the hand positions alone and a weak energy connection, you may be able to get a small amount of healing, but you can get so much more combining all the steps. You can harness the potential that lies within Reiki and allow it to manifest the changes you desire in your well-being.

So, this is how you can become better with Reiki: by using the system created by these steps to aid the realization of your healing intention. After laying the right foundation, you can then go further with aura cleansing, reiki breath, chakra balancing, etc.

With step 3, you set your healing intentions and formal message that is sent to your aura. This message details the kind of positive changes you want to see, and you transmit it by guiding the universal energy to your will.

While on the process, if you discover other issues while going about your aura scan, repeat steps 3 to 6 until the issues are taken off.

Now, you are going to learn how to close your Reiki connection safely with the next step.

Step 6: Close Your Connection

Reiki sessions shouldn't end without you taking this step. Reiki masters say that while they work with patients, they absorb the negative emotions of the patient and feel it lodged in their system.

You should ensure that the emotions are released from your body so that you can continue to enjoy a heightened state of energy. Again, you will have to rely on visualization to get this done by visualizing the energies being pulled out of your body through your palms and freeing your system.

Wash your hands afterwards in cold water, so they are purified and ensure that all residual energies are out entirely. Also, ensure that you are not in any way attached to the healing session emotionally. Believe that the energy is gone and take the last step below.

Step 7: Expand Your Energy Channels

Now, you have to consistently increase the channeling of your energy in between sessions so that your healing ability can be better in terms of effectiveness. This way, you will also be able to perform advanced techniques and progress to higher Reiki levels.

So, how can you expand your energy channels?

Firstly, you can utilize Ki exercises, which are meditations that you can practice by cycling energy through your system. These exercises open your chakras to allow more universal energy to get into your body and channeled towards healing.

Secondly, you can use attunements, which help you become harmonious with something. It is the primary way of advancing from the level of Reiki you are already in to another one. Attunement is like a radio dial; you only get a station when you turn into its frequency.

Most people can practice the primary forms of Reiki, so you need these exercises to be able to go over and beyond the fundamental level.

There will never be a better time to discover true happiness that happens as a result of the alignment you attain with your higher self. You know yourself best, you know the challenges you encounter daily, so if you want to experience some peace, now is the time to get on with Reiki healing.

You can use the ideas proffered in this chapter to embark on the most profound healing experience that will enable you to define your existence and live to your most accurate potentials.

Still, how does a Reiki session work? Do you know all about the positions of the hand and how distant Reiki treatment is done? To get answers to these questions and more, please flip over to the next chapter.

Chapter Three: How a Reiki Session Works

A Reiki session is quite an exciting experience because there are no typical sessions, set protocols, or length of time for all of them. Reiki healing can also be administered by anyone who has gone through training.

Healthcare providers, family members, or even you, after getting training, can use it to help someone else. There are also no typical settings for a Reiki session, although a quiet place is preferable.

Some people feel anxious about their Reiki session beforehand because, regardless of what they have read online or in books, they believe that nothing will ever prepare them for it than the experience itself. So, the objective of this chapter is to provide insight into how a Reiki session works so that you get an idea of the entire proceedings, know what to expect, and look forward to it with positive optimism.

You will also learn more about the traditional positions of hands, as well as the concept of self and distant Reiki healing.

For you to have a great experience, it is advised to choose a Reiki practitioner or friend who is well-trained at it and somehow you are comfortable with. It is crucial to feel good vibes with this person because, as you know, the universal energy cannot be forced.

The person you settle for should first describe the process and how he or she will structure the session to give you an idea of what to expect. Knowing what the individual will do next will be instrumental in keeping you relaxed and helping you build trust.

A Reiki session should take place in a quiet place where you wouldn't be disturbed or distracted. The professional Reiki practitioners have a dedicated space they use, and some may want to play instrumental music to mask out any noisy interference, but you can speak up if you prefer a silent room.

If you are going to receive Reiki in a hospital or nursing home, then it is possible that your session will be a shorter one (between 15 to 20 minutes). If you are taking the meeting in private, you can get up to 90 minutes per session (the time varies at the discretion of the practitioner's choice).

Now, what about the actual process? For some practitioners, an intake form is a part of their session as they use it to carry out a health interview, especially if the practitioner has some background training in health care or other forms of therapy. Meanwhile, others believe that Reiki is a form of folk practice instead of a healthcare solution; hence, they avoid using an intake form. For both types of practitioners, though, you may be required to sign a consent form, which is part of the standard practice.

After signing the consent or intake form, the professional will ask you some questions that give him or her insight into your specific needs while explaining the process. At this stage, being honest about how you feel is the surest way of getting the best out of the remaining part of the session.

So, try not to skip anything and be as transparent as you can by letting the professional know your needs, health conditions that you have been dealing with, and every other information that will give the practitioner more clarity regarding your case.

If you are taking the Reiki session in the hospital, the therapist may ask your permission to touch the painful areas as you explain. After this step, they will signal you to get ready for the session itself.

You will be required to lay on a table, fully clothed, or sit in a chair. Reiki will be offered through light touch that is non-invasive, with the practitioner's hand placed on the painful part of your body, as well as several other locations like your back, torso, head, etc. The placement of the practitioner's hand shouldn't be inappropriate or have too much pressure.

Moreover, there can be additional placements on your limbs if you have an old injury that still hurts. The practitioner can also hold their hands over an open wound or a burn as it is a way of offering Reiki to that injury. While all of this is going on, you may be wondering how you will be feeling or what you will experience during the sessions.

Some patients said that they felt refreshed or that they could think clearer in those moments. Others mentioned feeling like they were in a spa. Instead of a spa for the physical body, though, they were in a resort for the mind. At some point, you may feel like you are falling asleep or experience the same relaxed sensation that you get after a rewarding activity. These are some of the feelings people express during a Reiki session. Remember, it varies from one person to another.

Reiki experience is entirely subjective and often changeable. While it may be subtle for one person, it may be a fascinating experience for another person. Some people say they experience heat from the palms of the practitioner, which signals the flow of energy. For others, the practitioner's palms are relaxed. Another simplified Reiki session experience is that the patient feels subtle energy pulses as the practitioner's hands move over certain areas.

However, there is one feeling that cuts across most Reiki patients, and it is the feeling of comfort as recipients testify that they often feel like they are between the thresholds of consciousness (still being aware of their surroundings) and a sleep-like state that makes them as if they are meditating, even though they are not.

I know you probably think that there truly is a myriad of emotional experiences, and it all makes Reiki exciting and dramatic at the same time. With your first session, you may not get all of these feelings at once, but you will surely feel some release of stress and a sense of relaxation that makes you feel like you should come for another session.

Still, what's most interesting is the fact that, even after the session, you are bound to feel great afterwards. If you take on another meeting, your body gets used to it, and you can improve your aura while getting healed from the issues you have had.

The truth about Reiki is that it is mostly cumulative. Even if you don't feel anything at the beginning or with your first session, it doesn't dispute the fact that something has taken place within your body. It has been proven that people who do not get a mix of all of these experiences at first tend to have more profound experience later if they continue with the sessions.

Other notable changes that may consistently take place includes a sense of being poised, high reactivity, and better connection with the universe.

So, what should you do during the session?

After finding a great practitioner whom you are comfortable with, during the sessions, you can do a series of things, such as coming with the music you enjoy so that you can relax with familiar music while the expert does his or her work.

You can also use the restroom before the session so that you can lay comfortably without interruptions. If you are shy about being touched, ask the practitioner to show you the areas that he or she will reach during the meeting so that you can be mentally prepared and feel comfortable before it happens.

If you have trouble breathing while lying down, let the practitioner know before the session starts. If you had surgery, inform them about it as well so that they can float their hands over it or touch it tenderly. Pregnant women should also mention their condition before the session commences. For people who have digestive complaints, they may also have difficulty lying on their stomach, so the practitioner should be aware of it.

You will feel more relaxed during the session when the Reiki professional knows everything that they should know about you. You can ask for anything that will make you feel even more comfortable, such as a blanket or support under your knees. The practitioner will be there for you to make the process seamless and enjoyable for you.

When you start the session, don't just try to relax. Instead, do it for real.

Reiki is mostly a passive experience when the session starts as most of the work is done by the practitioner. At this point, you only need to enjoy the process and do nothing else.

Diagnosis is not a part of Reiki sessions when you are done with the practitioner. Nevertheless, some practitioners may have suggestions for you on following your body's needs, drinking more water, etc. Some people say that they leave a Reiki session feeling refreshed and then very tired afterward, and this is just the body's reaction to the natural healing process. On the evening of your first session, you will feel a sense of calm, have a good night sleep, and operate with mental clarity.

The number of sessions you are meant to have subsequently is determined by the practitioner, who may suggest a series of sessions afterward. The traditional recommendation is four sessions as it gives you ample opportunity to evaluate your benefits. You can discuss with the practitioner the ways through which you can spread the session to suit your needs or peculiar schedule.

If you have a very serious health condition, for instance, the practitioner may recommend that you take on four sessions in four consecutive days. However, you can choose to take it all as an advice and do what's best for you.

The Traditional Positions of the Hands

There cannot be a complete discourse on the impact and practice of Reiki without talking about the conventional positions of the hands. The hands are the medium through which energy flows. For any Reiki session to become successful, the practitioner must apply the right-hand usage for the right situation. There are several traditional hand positions, and we will take the time to present most of them later so that you can get acquainted with the motions that aid with Reiki success.

Below, you will gain access to 12 hand positions.

First Position: The Face

With this position, the hands are placed over the recipient's face, with the palms gently positioned on the forehead and fingers cupped tenderly over the eyes.

The position also allows the recipient to keep on breathing freely because the airways will be open as the practitioner ensures that there are no constrictions with the nose during the session.

Second Position: The Crown and Top of the Head

The wrist plays a pivotal role in this hand position as the practitioner uses the inner wrist to wrap his or her hands around the recipient's head. The fingertips will touch the ears for a more extensive feel.

Third Position: The Back of the Head

Here, the practitioner's hands will be gently tucked under the recipient's head while forming a cradle for the head. The back of the practitioner's hand will relax and rest on the table.

Fourth Position: Chin and Jawline

With this position, you get to surround the recipient's jawline with your hands while allowing your fingertips to touch underneath the chin and the heels of your hand near the recipient's ears.

Fifth Position: Neck, Collarbone, and Heart

While the patient is lying down, you will wrap your right hand lightly under his or her neck. If the recipient is uncomfortable with it, allow your hand to hover above the neck only. Then, stretch your left arm downwards and place your hand at the center of the heart.

Sixth Position: Ribs and Rib Cage

This hand position requires you to place your hand on the upper rib cage. Ensure that it is below the breast, though, because you are not supposed to touch private areas when treating someone, even if it's accidental.

Seventh Position: Abdomen

The practitioner's hand should be placed on the stomach, above the recipient's navel, close to the solar plexus area.

Eighth Position: Pelvic Bones

You need to place both palms over each pelvic bone.

Ninth Position: Shoulder Blades

Here, you will have to help the recipient change position from being on his or her back to lying on the stomach. Then, place your hands on the shoulder blades because it is a region that has a lot of emotional burdens. You have to keep your palms on the position longer so that you can dislodge the stuck energies.

Tenth Position: Mid-Back

The practitioner should place his or her hands on the middle area of the recipient's back.

Eleventh Position: Lower Back

Still on the back, you will use the hand position to get to the recipient's lower back region.

Twelfth Position: Sacrum

When the session is complete, the practitioner combs the recipient's aura with his or her hands to ensure that all energetic debris is cleared out. This debris may have come from the physical body during the session.

Also, you can make a silent request to the universe, saying that all negative energies should be transformed into positive ones!

We are still discovering more about how Reiki works, and we will be taking it a step further by learning how you can use Reiki as a self-treatment. It promises to be a fascinating sub-section, so keep on reading.

How Reiki Self-Treatment Works

Using self-treatment is an essential aspect of the Reiki healing program. If you can set aside 15 to 30 minutes daily to administer Reiki to yourself, you will be able to achieve a whole lot with your physical, emotional, and mental well-being.

Reiki self-treatment isn't different from the one done between a practitioner and a recipient as you will be utilizing your hand positions as well. When giving yourself Reiki, your vibration will go up, making it the perfect time for you to achieve all you set out to do in your life. You will also discover new habits, attitudes, creative ideas, and solutions on how you can handle life's pressing issues.

There are numerous ways to practice Reiki, but all of these, regardless of the variants, must be done practically. After all, Reiki is never done in the abstract. If you settle for a system that works for yourself, it will become easier for you to practice daily, get better at it, and make it a part of your life.

Before you decide on doing Reiki self-treatment, you must seek out the challenges you are having and have an honest discussion with yourself about them, just like you would do with a practitioner. Armed with information on what you need help with, you can take on the path towards self-treatment and get a cure.

You can start with self-practice by concentrating on these critical areas: throat, lower rib, navel, back of the head, the crown of the head, face, throat, and lower abdomen. You can lay on your side with a pillow, doubled over, and then stay on your back to get it done.

Your practice time should be synchronized with your schedule. Don't just stick to anyone's schedule that you have seen online; seek out what works for you instead and use it. If it is in the morning, then you should do it as soon as you wake up before opening your eyes.

Let your hands spread to the parts of your body that you want to work with. As you savor the energy, allow yourself to be drawn into the experience. At the end of your sessions, linger a bit in bed to complete it, then wash your hands and drink lots of water before embarking on your day.

Organize Your Practice

If you like to have intervals in between, that's your choice as well. You can use a timer to signal the breaks you will take or download Reiki timer apps on your mobile device. Also, introduce a protocol to your self-treatment as it helps your hand to create a habit of doing so without thinking. The more you practice, the more natural it becomes for your hand positions.

Remember to prop yourself up in a very comfortable position as well so that you are not focused on your body but your experience. Don't rely on random times during the day to practice or when the chosen time comes to use your hand positions to administer healing.

Now, there will be days when it feels like you cannot be consistent. Don't beat yourself up about it and ensure that you are not putting too much pressure on yourself. Instead of rushing for 30 to 40 minutes to practice the routine, you can start with 10 minutes and gradually build it up. After all, a little practice is better than none at all.

Use the pattern: Practice-observe-contemplate-repeat!

How Distant Reiki Treatment Works

A lot of people are unsure about the concept of remote Reiki sessions, and it is easy to understand their skepticism because one can only marvel at the possibility of being able to transfer healing to someone else in another place through this process. How can someone else in another room, city, or country experience heal from a Reiki practitioner, right?

Well, we have already established the fact that Reiki uses healing energy, and it cannot be contained or confined to a room. Within our material world, we must do everything in person, e.g., go shopping, walk the dog, etc. However, these are physical activities that are made through the body, and they do not make use of Reiki.

Reiki can be holistically used to restore the balance to a person's body, mind, and spirit. It can also promote the regenerative abilities of the universal energy because it goes beyond the physical. We have the power inside our body, and this energy has its vibrations, which creates a field around us, a.k.a. the energy field.

Four Fields of Energy

Energy fields can be felt through touch. This is the reason why Reiki is performed with the hands.

We have the emotional field, which is where we feel. It extends from 1 to 3 inches from the physical body.

There is the physical field, which is the first layer. It stays ¼ to 2 inches from the body.

We also have the mental field that is known for aiding our mental processes and thoughts. It can be sensed at 3 to 8 inches from the body.

The spiritual field consists of about four or more layers, helps us stay attuned to our spiritual reality, and extends by 6 to 20 inches beyond the body.

How to Do Distance Healing

You will use the energy fields to send healing to someone else in another place, and they will receive it. However, how can you do that?

First, you must ensure that your hands and chakras are empowered with the Power symbol. Then, you need to apply Reiki to yourself for about 10 to 15 minutes. Next, you will need to invoke the distance healing symbols (remember what we discussed on symbols) and say the person's name three times.

While repeating their name, visualize the individual whom you want to send healing to and get ready to send the universal energy to each of their field levels.

If you want to send energy to a person's physical level, for instance, start by imagining it entering their chakra and then going inside their body and gently filling them up. As it happens, the organs in their bodies are also getting the vibration. Then, the energy starts to radiate. You see them glow with this energy and expand it as the different fields are full.

After sending healing to their physical field, you should also do the same to their emotional area next. You can do this by imagining them getting filled with so much joy, peace, satisfaction, and great well-being. Visualize the glow from their physical field getting into the emotional field.

Then, you can send universal energy to their mental field by intending for their thoughts to be very calm. They know what to do because their brain is working and the ideas are flowing smoothly. Now, imagine that they are getting solutions to their problems, believe that they are no longer worried, and Reiki is filling them up with high energy for their mental field.

Next, you will have to send energy to their spiritual field by visualizing it filling up their spirit and causing restoration. Visualize a renewal of their soul, mind, and essence as the flow of energy remains the direct link from where they are to heaven.

Your intention should be for them to be filled with spiritual energy beyond their being. As they feel everything, they should be able to embrace this new spiritual height that will transform their lives.

Now, before you do all of these, you must have a conversation with the individual who needs help. To be precise, ask them questions about each level and intentionally learn more about their challenges.

Don't ask vague questions; be direct by starting with each field. You can get to know how the patients are feeling emotionally if they are happy or sad to gain access to their emotional area. Then, try to find out if they have any pain in their bodies for the physical field.

Are they worried about something? Are they restless when sleeping? These are questions for the mental field. Ask them how their spirit feels and if they feel unsafe in the world as well for their spiritual field.

The fact that you know their issues doesn't mean that you get to perform Reiki immediately, though. Start by preparing them for it. Tell them to get ready for healing and that they should allow the universal energy to heal them. Then, you can do it for 10 to 20 minutes on each field level.

When the session is over, tell them to rest and visualize the Power symbol over them. Disconnect from their energy field by dry bathing, give yourself a few minutes of Reiki, and call them afterward to know how they are doing and what they have experienced. Always end all distant Reiki sessions with gratitude for the healing process.

Distant Reiki healing became very popular and essential when people realized that they didn't have to go through the stress of traveling from one country to another to get help. The time spent trying to book an appointment or meet a practitioner could be channeled into other productive things instead. More importantly, distant Reiki makes it possible for the recipient to be comfortable at home.

Some people may not feel free in an office or a Reiki space far from home. When they get the freedom to do it in their place, therefore, it adds a lot of value to the process for them. One-on-one sessions can also be much more expensive than distant healing.

So, getting Reiki from a distance is an excellent alternative to having a one-on-one session, which can be a source of inconvenience to a lot of people. Most individuals who have never practiced distant Reiki often end up preferring it after experiencing it for the first time because they get the same results as though they were in the same room with the practitioner.

Nonetheless, the only way to know if it works for you is to try it out yourself. Make sure it is scheduled for a time that you prefer and that you are in a quiet place, focused and ready to receive healing.

With distant Reiki, you don't have to work around someone else's schedule. You can also record the details of your healing while taking note of what works in which field, as well as what areas need more work.

Reiki sessions are the connecting dots between you and the healing you anticipate. As such, being prepared for it is essential. We have used this chapter to provide concise information that will prepare you for the Reiki sessions. While you may be looking forward to everything mentioned here in terms of the experience, you should know that no two sessions are the same.

Keep an open mind, enjoy the process, and love the experience it brings as this is the only way you can have a personalized Reiki experience! We are moving on to one of the most exciting parts of our journey as it deals with a question most people can't stop asking, "What ailment or disease can Reiki cure?"

Let's find out in the next section, shall we?

Chapter Four: Ailments Healed With Reiki

One of the reasons why there is a lot of emphasis on Reiki treatment in the world today is that there are more success stories shared about their impact. Hence, many people are willing to not only give it a try but also become consistent with it.

Now, if you have never tried Reiki before, and this book is your first encounter with the subject matter, you would want to know the benefits you stand to gain by adopting this approach. After all, there are so many options available online, so one can only wonder what's so special about Reiki.

If you have practiced Reiki in the past or had prior knowledge about this healing process, then you must be curious to unearth the actual illnesses and diseases that Reiki can cure. This chapter will show you the types of conditions that can be treated with Reiki and explain how you can achieve the desired results with proper hand positions. We already covered the aspect of self-treatment, so you know what to do already if you want to administer it to yourself.

Not all Reiki sessions or treatment patterns are suitable for all diseases and illnesses. Before embarking on a treatment process, therefore, you will need to know the specific condition you are dealing with, as well as the kind of session and hand position to use. Let's discuss that briefly before getting right on to the types of illnesses that Reiki can cure.

There are specific positions of the entire body treatment with Reiki that is meant for specific symptoms. Such positions can be used for a longer time during the healing process. For such complaints, you only require quick yet consistent sessions. For example, chronic illnesses can be cured after four consecutive sessions. If there will be an extension, the seriousness of the disease will determine it.

Others may take a while before achieving immediate healing, primarily if we are talking about cancer in which weekly meetings may be required. The recipient will have to be patient and ensure that there is enough connection with all Reiki sessions for maximum effect.

For diseases that cause disfiguration of the body, the recipient will need to balance his or her second and fifth chakras. If they are dealing with life-threatening illnesses, they will have to focus on the fifth and sixth chakras.

If a person is dealing with paralysis or a form of impairment, then he or she should work on balancing the first, third, and fifth chakras. Reiki treatments are useful for illnesses that involve the nervous system and the mind.

Most importantly, you must know that Reiki treatment is not a substitute for consultation with a physician. It is not an alternative for psychotherapy or natural therapy sessions either. If you find that you are increasingly worried about your state and you cannot stick to Reiki sessions, then you must consult a medical practitioner or visit a hospital.

Different Illnesses Reiki Treatment Can Cure

Please note that all solutions proffered below are also presented with the kind of hand positions that you can use to achieve the desired results. It isn't all about placing your hands on a person's body; you must transfer universal energy. If you are the recipient, the practitioner will do the same.

Now, the reason why most diseases are listed together in one section is that ailments and the Reiki treatment required have similar hand positions.

Headache and Backache

With headaches, one position doesn't apply for all at once, so you can try everything and stick to whichever is most effective.

First Position

The first step is to place your hand in a parallel position from the forehead to the region of the top teeth and then to the right and left of the nose.

Second Position

The practitioner's hands should cup the back of the recipient's head with his or her fingertips placed on the medulla oblongata. This is the soft spot along the midline of the head to the neck and halfway to where the hard bone ends and changes into a soft depression.

Third Position

The healer's hands should be placed between the shoulders and shoulder blades.

Fourth Position

The hands should remain on the shoulder blades at this point.

Fifth Position

The hands should then be on the soles of the feet. Specifically, the big toes have to be covered from the tips.

Backache

You can add local backache treatment to the hand Reiki positions below.

First Position

The practitioner should place his or her hands in a parallel position from the forehead to top teeth region and then to the right and left of the nose.

Second Position

The hands should now be on the shoulders and shoulder blades.

Third Position

Place the hands on the shoulder blades.

Fourth Position

The hands should cover the hollows of the knees.

Fifth Position

The hands should then be on the soles of the recipient's feet. Specifically, the big toes have to be covered from the tips.

Kidney and Liver Problems

First Position

The healer should place hands in a parallel position from the forehead to the region of the top teeth in an identical position to the right and left of the nose.

Second Position

The balls of the thumbs should be on the ridges of the pelvic bones. The tips of the hands should be close to each other at the pubic bone, forming a V.

Third Position

Place the hands on the lower ribs, right above the kidney.

Fourth Position

Place one hand on the sacral plate and the other one vertically below it with little pressure.

Fifth Position

Place the hands around the ankles.

Liver Complaints

First Position

One hand should be placed on the lowest ribs (right side) with another hand below it.

Second Position

Place one hand above the navel. Keep the other hand underneath it.

Third Position

Place the hands on the shoulder blades.

Arthritis, Pain, and Fractures

Arthritis

First Position

The hands of the healer should be on the lower ribs, above the kidney.

Second Position

The hands should then be on the soles of the feet. Specifically, the big toes have to be covered from the tips.

Pain

First Position

Place your hands between the shoulders and shoulder blades.

Second Position

The hands should now be placed on the shoulder blades. If the patient is complaining about bone pain, one hand should be put above and below the main cervical vertebra at the neck's nape.

If it is a pain in the hips and legs, the universal energy should be channeled to the entire back and outside the hips.

For arm pain, Reiki can be applied to the top of the shoulder with the positions below.

First Position

The hands should be placed between the shoulders and shoulder blades.

Second Position

The hands should stay on the shoulder blades.

Fractures

Reiki treatment needs to be performed regularly after the bones are set up with the hand positions below.

First Position

The practitioner should place one hand from the forehead to the region of the top teeth in a parallel position to the right and left of the nose.

Second Position

One hand should be placed gently on the lowest ribs and another one directly below it.

Third Position

With one hand on the sacral plate, the other hand should be placed vertically below with a little more pressure.

Fourth Position

The healer should place hands on the soles of the feet with the big toes covered from the tips.

Diabetes, Asthma, and Heart Attack

Diabetes

For Reiki treatment with diabetes, the elbows should receive a lot of concentration with the positions below.

First Position

The healer should place hands from the forehead to the region of the top teeth in a parallel position to the right and left sides of the nose.

Second Position

Hands should be placed on the left lower ribs and below it.

Third Position

The healer should place one hand across the thymus while the other hand is at a right angle below and between the breasts, forming a T.

Fourth Position

The hands are placed at the soles of the feet with the big toes covered from the tips.

Asthma

First Position

The healer's hands should cup the back of the recipient's head with fingertips place don the Medulla oblongata.

Second Position

The practitioner should place his or her hands in a parallel position to the right and the left of the nose. This should be done from the forehead to the region of the top teeth.

Third Position

With one hand placed across the thymus, the other hand should be at the right angle and between the breasts, forming a T.

Fourth Position

Place the balls of the thumb on the ridges of the pelvic bone with the tips of the hands close to each other at the pubic bone, forming a V.

Heart Attack

If a person has a heart attack, the doctors should be called immediately. However, before the medical experts come, Reiki can be administered to the upper and lower abdomen. Remember that the energy of the universe should not be given directly to the heart.

First Position

Place one hand on the right side of the lowest ribs while the other hand goes underneath it.

Second Position

One hand should be placed above the navel and the other hand below it.

Third Position

The healer's hand should go between the shoulders and shoulder blades.

Fourth Position

The hands should be placed on the lower ribs, above the kidneys.

For general heart trouble, consult a physician before taking any other form of healing.

Epileptic Fits and Weight Problem

Epileptic Fits

For epileptic fits, the universal energy should flow into the spine between the shoulder blades. The sessions should only take place before or after a seizure.

First Position

The healer's hand should cup the back of the recipient's head with his or her fingertips placed on the medulla oblongata.

Second Position

The hands should cover the front section of the neck, avoiding making contact with it.

Third Position

One hand has to stay above the navel with the other hand below it.

Weight Problem

First Position

From the forehead region of the top teeth, the practitioner should place his or her hands in a parallel position to the left and right of the nose.

Second Position

The hands should cover the front section of the neck without touching it so that the recipient feels comfortable.

Third Position

Place one hand above the navel, while the other hand goes below it.

Fourth Position

Use the ball of the thumbs on the ridges of the pelvic bones with the tips of the hands close to each other at the pubic bone, forming a V.

Fifth Position

Place the hands on the shoulder blades.

Sixth Position

One hand has to be placed across the sacral plate while the other one stays vertically below with a little bit more pressure.

Seventh Position

The hands are placed around the ankles.

Anemia

Anemia can be taken care of with the universal energy channeled at the top of the head using the positions below.

First Position

With the hands cupping the back of the head, the fingertips should be placed on the medulla oblongata.

Second Position

One hand should be placed on the lowest ribs on the right side, while the other is underneath it.

Third Position

Place your hands on the left lower rib and then below it.

Cancer and Fever

For cancer, it is crucial to perform regular treatment for the entire body while channeling the hand positions that you will find below with universal energy.

First Position

With one hand on the lowest ribs on the right side, the other hand can be placed below it.

Second Position

One hand should be placed above the navel and the other hand goes below it.

Third Position

The practitioner should place one hand across the thymus while the other is at the right angle below and between the breasts, forming a T. The total duration for this position should be between 15 to 20 minutes.

There can be cases in which the cancer patient is extremely weak. In this situation, it is vital to balance the chakras. The hand positions below will be helpful.

For Frail Recipients

First Position

One hand should be placed across the sacral plate and the other hand goes vertically below it with no pressure.

Second Position

The hands are placed at the soles of the feet with the big toes covered from the tips.

Tongue Cancer

For tongue cancer, Reiki has to be channeled in the body from the feet. If it is breast or urogenital cancer, it matters to do intensive Reiki at the second chakra with particular attention paid to the hand positions below.

First Position

The balls of the thumb should be on the ridges of the pelvis while the tips of the hands should be placed close to each other at the pubic bone, forming a V.

Second Position

One hand is placed across the sacral plate with the other hand goes vertically below with no pressure.

Third Position

The hands are placed around the ankles.

Leukemia

For leukemia, Reiki treatment should be used for the whole body, and the recommended positions below are excellent.

First Position

The healer should place one hand on the lowest ribs on the right side while the other hand is directly underneath it.

Second Position

The hands should be placed on the lower left ribs and then below it.

Third Position

The balls of the thumb should be placed on the ridges of the pelvic bones while the tips of the hands should be close to each other at the pubic bone, forming a V.

Fourth Position

With one hand placed across the sacral plate, the other hand should be placed vertically below it with no pressure.

Fifth Position

The practitioner's hands should be placed around the ankles.

Sixth Position

The hands should be placed on the soles of the feet with the big toes covered from the tips.

Fever

First Position

From the forehead region of the top teeth, the practitioner should place his or her hands in a parallel position to the right and left of the nose.

Second Position

The hands should be placed on the recipient's ears.

Third Position

The hands should be covering the front section of the neck without touching it.

Fourth Position

Place the hands on the left lower ribs and below it.

Fifth Position

Place one hand across the thymus and the other hand at a right angle position below and between the breasts. Let both hands form a T. Now, there can be a temporary surge of temperature when this is applied, but it will be followed swiftly by great relief.

Cramps and Leg Problems

Cramps

Cramps can be very discomforting, and the most common ones take place in the leg area. Hence, this section will present the hand positions that you can use to achieve Reiki treatment for and leg problems.

First Position

The hands should be placed in a parallel manner from the forehead to the region of the top teeth and then right and left of the nose.

Second Position

The healer's hands should be on the lowest ribs on the right side and then below it.

Third Position

The hands are placed on the shoulder blades.

Fourth Position

Place the hands on the lower ribs, above the kidney.

Fifth Position

The hands should cover the hollows of the knee.

Sixth Position

The hands should be placed on the soles of the feet with the big toes covered from the tips.

Leg Problems

First Position

Hands should be placed from the forehead region of the top teeth and to the parallel position of the right and left sides of the nose.

Second Position

One hand should be across the sacral plate, while the other hand is placed vertically below with no pressure.

Third Position

The hands should cover the hollows of the recipient's knee.

Fourth Position

For the fourth position, the hands should be placed around the ankles.

Fifth Position

Place the hands on the soles of the feet with the big toes covered from the tips.

Blood Pressure and Bleeding

The positions you will find below will aid the Reiki treatment for bleeding, as well as high or low blood pressure.

Bleeding

If you notice that the bleeding is severe and consistent, then you will need to administer first aid. However, for small bleedings, Reiki can be used to heal the wound.

First Position

The healer should place his or her hands from the forehead to the region of the upper teeth in a parallel position from the right to left nose.

Second Position

The hands should cover the front section of the neck to pass on universal energy without touching the neck.

Third Position

The practitioner's hands should be on the lower side of the left ribs and below it.

Fourth Position

The hands are to be placed on the lower ribs, above the kidney.

Fifth Position

The hands should cover the hollows of the knee.

High Blood Pressure

First Position

The hands should be placed on the front section of the neck. As always, try not to apply too much pressure or touch the neck.

Second Position

Place the hands on the lower side of the left ribs and below it.

Third Position

The hands should be at the soles of the feet with the big toes covered from the tips.

Low Blood Pressure

First Position

The practitioner's hands are to be placed between the shoulders and shoulder blades.

Second Position

Move the hands on the shoulder blades. Hold this position for a while.

Third Position

With one hand on the sacral plate, the other hand can be placed vertically below it with more pressure.

Fourth Position

Place the hands on the soles of the feet, and the big toes should be covered from the tips.

Detoxification

The Reiki treatment for detoxification requires sessions for the entire body until signs of healing start to show forth. Some of them include darker urine with a different smell, better bowel movements, and sweating. The recipient should also have a regular intake of water, lots of rest periods, and showers.

If you are experiencing challenges with your liver, then you need to consult a physician for proper medical checks.

First Position

The healer should place his or her hands from the forehead to the region of the top teeth in a parallel position, moving to the right and left of the nose.

Second Position

This position should be done on the neck, and it works directly on thyroid and parathyroid gland, as well as on the larynx, vocal cords, and lymph nodes.

Third Position

Place one hand on the lowest ribs on the right side. Put the other hand below it, too.

Fourth Position

One hand should be placed on the lower side of the left ribs and below it.

Fifth Position

Place one hand on the navel and the other below it.

Sixth Position

One hand should be placed across the thymus while the other is at a right angle below and between the breasts, forming a T.

Seventh Position

The balls of the thumb should be placed on the ridges of the pelvic bones with the tips of the hands close to each other at the pubic bone, forming a V.

Eight Position

The hands should be placed on the lower ribs, above the kidney.

Ninth Position

With one hand placed across the sacral plate, the other hand should be vertically below it with more pressure.

Tenth Position

The hands should be placed on the soles of the feet, and the big toes should be covered from the tips.

Bladder Problems and Acne

Bladder Problems

These positions will work well with you if you experience severe bladder problems.

First Position

The practitioner should cup the back of the recipient's head with the fingertips placed on the medulla oblongata.

Second Position

The balls of the thumb are placed on the ridges of the pelvic bones with the tips of the hands close to each other at the pubic bone, forming a V.

Third Position

Place the hands between the shoulders and the shoulder blades.

Fourth Position

One hand goes across the sacral plate, and the other is placed below it vertically with increased pressure.

Fifth Position

The hands should be placed around the knees.

Acne

For acne, the Reiki treatment should begin with the whole body for a few days. Then, the following sessions should be done with more focus on the affected area.

First Position

The hands should cover the neck (front section) while being careful to avoid causing any discomfort to the recipient.

Second Position

The hands are placed on the lower ribs, above the kidney.

Third Position

The practitioner should place one hand on the lowest ribs on the right side and the other hand underneath it.

Fourth Position

Next, one hand is placed on the navel and the other below it.

Fifth Position

For the last position, the balls of the thumb should be placed on the ridges of the pelvic bones with the tips of the hands close to each other at the pubic bone, forming a V.

Rheumatism

First Position

One hand should be placed above the navel with the other below it.

Second Position

The balls of the thumb should be placed on the ridges of the pelvic bones with the tips of the hands close to each other at the pubic bone, forming a V.

Third Position

The hands are to be placed on the lower ribs, above the kidney.

Fourth Position

The hands should cover the hollows of the knee.

Menstrual Complaints and Childbirth

First Position

One hand should be on the lowest ribs on the right side with the other directly below it.

Second Position

One hand is placed above the navel and the other goes below it.

Third Position

The balls of the thumb should be placed on the ridges of the pelvic bones with the tips of the hands close to each other at the pubic bone, forming a V.

Fourth Position

The hands should be placed on the shoulder blades.

Fifth Position

With one hand across the sacral plate, the other hand should be placed below in a vertical position with a bit more pressure.

Sixth Position

The hands should be placed around the ankles.

Seventh Position

The hands should be placed on the soles of the feet, and the big toes should be covered from the tips.

Childbirth

Reiki can help expectant mothers enjoy a relaxing experience that makes the process of childbirth easier. It also aids the opening of the pelvis, which makes the delivery less painful. However, the following hand positions must be used before the D-day.

First Position

One hand should be placed above the navel and the other below it.

Second Position

The healer should place the balls of the thumb on the pelvic bones with the tips close to each other at the pubic bone, forming a V.

Third Position

The hands should be placed on the lower ribs, above the kidney.

Fourth Position

One hand should be placed across the sacral plate, which is the bone plate above the fold of the buttocks. The other hand should be placed below it vertically with a little bit of pressure for easy contact with universal energy.

Nose Complaints

In addition to the hand positions that you will utilize for this ailment, you should also use local treatment. The ones you will find below are for three forms of noise-related health challenges that cut across nosebleeds, sinus problems, and nose blockages.

Nose Blockage

First Position

A healer should place hands in a parallel position to the right and left of the nose from the forehead to the region of the top teeth.

Second Position

One hand should be placed on the lowest ribs on the right side, with the other hand directly below.

Third Position

With one hand placed across the thymus, the other hand should be at a right angle below and between the breasts, forming a T.

Sinus Problem

For sinus problems, use the positions above, along with the ones you will find below.

First Position

The balls of the thumb should be placed on the pelvic ridges with the tips of the hands close to each other at the pubic bone, forming a V.

Second Position

The hands should then be placed on the shoulder blades.

Third Position

One hand should be placed across the sacral plate which is the bone plate just above the folds of the buttocks and the other hand placed in a vertical position below. This time, however, there should be a little more pressure.

Fourth Position

The hands should be placed around the ankles.

Nosebleed

First Position

The hands should cup the back of the head with fingertips placed on the medulla oblongata. Ensure that your fingertips are on the soft spot that you can feel when they are passed along the midline of the head to the neck. This should be where half the hard bone ends (that's how you locate the medulla oblongata).

Second Position

The hands should cover the front section of the neck. With this position, the universal energy will lead to the nasal organ as the nose is firmly connected to the throat.

Third Position

One hand should be placed above the navel and the other hand below it.

Fourth Position

The hands should be placed between the shoulders and shoulder blades.

Fifth Position

Finally, place the hands alone on the shoulder blades and release the universal energy.

Cold, Cough, Insomnia, and Allergies

Common cold can lead to several other issues if left unchecked. When you have insomnia, after all, there is a higher possibility of various diseases settling in your body because you don't get good sleep, which is a requirement for a healthy and robust body. Allergies can also be very discomforting. However, with the right Reiki hand positions, you can get a cure for all three issues.

Cold

First Position

The healer should place his or her hands from the forehead to the areas around the top teeth and the left side of the nose.

Second Position

The hands should cover the front section of the neck, but the healer should avoid touching the neck directly as it can lead to discomfort and fear in some people.

Third Position

One hand should be placed across the thymus and the other hand at the right angle below and between the breasts, forming a T. This position channels the Reiki's healing energy into the recipient's body with each hand movement.

Insomnia

For insomnia, channeling Reiki to the collarbone is highly effective.

First Position

The hands should be placed in a parallel position to the right and left side of the nose from the forehead to the region of the top teeth.

Second Position

Place the hands on the temples with fingertips getting to the cheekbones.

Third Position

One hand should be placed above the navel and the other one below it.

Fourth Position

The balls of the practitioner's thumb should be placed on the ridges of the pelvic bones, and the tips of the hands should be close to each other at the pubic bone, forming a V.

Allergies

Whole-body treatment is usually the beginning of a Reiki treatment for allergies, with a focus on the specific regions where the reactions manifest.

First Position

The hands should cover the front section of the neck, but do not touch the neck.

Second Position

The hands should be placed in a parallel position to the left and right sides of the nose from the forehead to the top teeth region.

Third Position

The balls of the thumb should be placed on the ridges of the pelvic bones with the tips of the hands close to each other at the pubic bone, creating a V.

Fourth Position

One hand should be placed above the navel and the other hand below it.

Give the recipient a few minutes to rest after each session and monitor health progress closely to decide on a continuance with sessions and the duration for the meetings.

When we say that the world is beginning to adopt the Reiki approach for treatment, the content of this chapter has provided insight into the reasons for their interest. Reiki truly has immense potential. The more you learn about its abilities, the more exciting it gets because there are layers to unravel with every session. Not to mention, it gets better with time.

Nevertheless, there are also additional benefits to using Reiki for treatment purposes. We just concentrated on the aspect of illnesses and diseases in this chapter. In the next chapter, we will take you through the other perks that will touch your mind, as well as your emotional balance.

Chapter Five: Additional Benefits of Reiki

Isn't it amazing that we have probably embarked on this journey with you knowing little or nothing about Reiki, and now you know not only what it is about but also how to administer it as a practitioner and receive it as a recipient?

The journey with this book only validates the fact that there is so much to unearth about Reiki. The more you learn, the more you want to discover about it. We have built solid foundations that have created an enabling environment for understanding all things, but we are ready to take things up a notch.

Most of the information you will find everywhere else about Reiki focuses solely on the health benefits that individuals can enjoy. By saying 'health' here, we are referring to physical relief from illnesses and diseases.

However, there is so much more to Reiki than that. Of course, it is essential that we seek such help, but wouldn't it be great if we expand our knowledge about it?

When we started, I told you that this is a comprehensive book that doesn't just cover the basics of the subject matter but also goes deeper to present information about Reiki. Hence, in this chapter, we are going to consider its other benefits that don't focus on illnesses alone.

Through this chapter, you will realize that Reiki is a treatment option that offers so much more to you with a few sessions. The perks that you will find here are not similar to the ones that we have discussed in the previous section. They do not come with hand positions either.

You will get to learn another approach to weighing in on the benefits that Reiki provides. You will also realize that the treatment goes beyond what happens to your body and cuts across what occurs inside it, as well as in your mind.

Additional Psychological and Mental Benefits of Reiki

Accelerates Self-Healing Ability

Reiki healing makes it easier for your body to return to its natural state of being able to heal itself from within. This is made possible by the life force energy associated with Reiki.

Your body starts to move in the right direction as your breathing, heart rate, and blood pressure improves. When you self-treat with Reiki or get healing from someone else, one of the first activities that you will do during every session is to breathe deeply. When you practice and perfect deep breathing, your mind will get settled naturally.

As your respiration gets stronger, your body opens up to receive new energy and expels the negative one. The process of being able to do so can accelerate your body's self-healing abilities as it is a correctional process with long-term mental and psychological benefits.

The body was created to self-heal, but it started to lose its natural touch when we exposed our mind and thought processes to contradictory ideas. So, for you to return to that natural state of self-healing, you must introduce something from the universe again. This is where Reiki becomes very powerful.

The more universal energy you are exposed to, the more you can strike a balance with your natural self-healing state. So, instead of you falling ill all the time, you may stronger, optimistic about life, and energized to do more.

Gets Rid of Bad Karma

Bad karma is likened to a blockage in your system. Now, when your artery is blocked, the blood flow to your heart is reduced, and it may lead to a cardiac arrest. This explanation with blood flow perfectly captures the situation that goes on in your life when you have bad karma around you. You start to feel like your energy and will to live a better life is trapped. With the manifestation of adverse events, you tend to believe that life is unfair.

You will also believe that the reason why other people seem to have a more comfortable life is that the universe favors them more than you. Get rid of lousy karma using the universal energy and avoid getting trapped energy. After all, the latter manifests through depression, irritability, and other forms of physical problems.

Reiki helps in cleansing your karma, and the blockages can be removed by a Reiki master as he or she can channel the energy of the universe through themselves into your body to cleanse the bad karma surrounding you.

When bad karma is taken care of, you will feel that the energy around you is better and that you have been empowered to live your life to its fullest potential. If you keep up with the Reiki sessions, then you will get rid of it forever!

Improves Quality of Life

When we talk about the quality of life, we do not only refer to how you live in terms of the material things, e.g., your home, cars, clothes, etc. We are more focused on the quality of your daily experiences. What you go through every day eventually sums up the kind of life you are generally living.

If most of your days are challenge-ridden, you can easily overcome so many issues that leave you feeling less motivated in the long run. Then, there is a problem somewhere. It means that there are negative energies that have crept into your consciousness and are making it difficult for you to embrace the good stuff in your life.

With universal energy, not only can you embrace the good things you have going for yourself, but you also get to become aware of them and intentionally focus on it instead of being worried about what isn't working.

There will be things that you will surely have to deal with, such as personal challenges, but you don't need to make these things the center of your existence. Allow the quality of your life get an improvement with universal energy; let your chakras and bodily energies become aligned towards one goal, which is being the best version of yourself and living your best life today.

After Reiki sessions, you will realize that the good things you can do to add some quality into your life aren't so tricky at all. Concentrate on the little things, smile a lot, and seek happiness from within. All of this can be made possible with consistent exposure to the universal energy.

Improves Sleep

A significant outcome when you receive Reiki is relaxation, which aids you in getting better sleep. We become strong enough to combat fatigue and other illnesses attributed to a lack of quality sleep this way.

We mentioned earlier that some Reiki recipients fall asleep during sessions, but it doesn't end with the Reiki meetings. A few of them continue that way after the sessions because they have received a renewed energy that keeps them at peace with themselves.

The thoughts and issues that keep you awake at night enough not to get good sleep can be taken care of with universal energy. One of the significant aims of Reiki is to empower you with the inner energy that your body requires for self-care.

So, you wouldn't need to actively do a lot of things on your own as there is an energy force within you now that causes everything else about your life to align correctly, even your sleep patterns. If you have been struggling with getting the recommended hours of sleep or you have discovered that you cannot stay in bed throughout the night, then you need Reiki sessions.

If you think that by doing nothing about this sleep deprivation challenge you are helping yourself as you hope, you need to rethink your actions. Why do you think people take sleeping pills? When you have a sleep issue, you don't sit and wait it out. Instead, you do something!

In this case, you wouldn't have to take pills or resort to other forms of drugs that you may have to enjoy the Reiki process and bask in the feel of it while getting better sleep subsequently.

Promotes Spiritual Growth and Emotional Cleansing

People erroneously believe that they need to be into spirituality before they can enjoy the benefits of Reiki, and this isn't true. You don't need to be an enthusiastic, spiritual being before taking in the universal energy.

When you experience spiritual growth, you will notice that it does so much more for your mind as you will feel at peace with yourself more and be contented with life. Reiki doesn't only address specific issues; it also focuses on the whole person. So, when you go for sessions, feeling less wholesome spiritually, you can be sure of experiencing a subtle shift from deep within your being.

Suddenly you have guidance on what to do, you are inspired to make attitudinal changes for the better, and your take on situations are better framed from a fresh perspective instead of the normal thought processes you imbibed in the past.

Listen, sometimes you don't need a lot of people giving you advice, what you need is to have an improved inner conviction that helps you make decisions and stand boldly with the choice you made because you know you did the correct thing.

So now, other people can come to you for emotional advice as well because you have gotten your life together and you are leaning more on the spiritual energy acquired from Reiki instead of your intuition. Emotional cleansing makes it possible for you to overlook the wrongs of those who hurt you and move on gracefully because you know your life isn't defined by how you feel about others.

A lot of people who complain about some fundamental mental issues need to experience emotional cleansing, and they will be fine. Let the universal energy protect your mind from adverse emotional reactions and help you see beyond the pain or hurt you may feel.

Speeds Up Recovery From Illnesses and Surgeries

If you discover that it always takes you a long time to recover from diseases and operations, then you will need universal energy. Reiki speeds up recovery from illnesses and surgeries as the periods after treatment can be a very complicated one that, if not properly managed, may cause the individual to experience a relapse.

For some people, the reason why they are unable to recover swiftly may be because of the side effects of drugs and surgical procedures. However, Reiki can help them adjust to the medicine or treatment that they are given by reducing the impact of side effects.

If you have had surgery recently, wait for a few days and then take on a Reiki session to solidify the healing process. You may not have to take on more than one session because you are also taking drugs or other forms of medicine. After the first one, though, discuss your feelings with the healer so that he or she can ascertain if you will need more sessions.

After a medical treatment, your body may still be trying to normalize again, which means that it needs support. To be specific, it needs a life force energy that can enhance the impact of the treatment that you have received.

After your Reiki session, you will notice that whatever pain you felt after surgery or treatment is gone or has subsided, it is mainly because of the impact of universal energy. The same way Reiki helps new mothers after delivery gets better is how it helps others regain their health and vitality.

You don't need more drugs to take care of your post-surgery or post-treatment period. What you need is an energy force field that moves through your body, recreating a stronger response to the medical procedures you have gone through.

Guarantees Mental Freedom

A lot of people are physically free, but they are not mentally free. Hence, they deal with an inner self-identity struggle that sets them in a prison of the mind. "I feel free" is often the statement made by Reiki recipients after their sessions. Some individuals may not even be able to describe this feeling aptly, but they know that something was taken away, and something more powerful released inside them.

The concept of mental freedom isn't discussed well enough because some people do not even know it exists. They are not familiar with the idea; that's why they don't know when they are mentally free and when they are not. The inability to make your own decisions and seek the validation of others makes you feel mentally caged.

Reiki can help you regain freedom through exciting sessions that make it possible for you to feel empowered and comfortable with yourself enough to trust your decisions. A person who is mentally free doesn't need to prove anything to anyone.

In the social media-inspired world we live in today, if a person can stay true to themselves, that individual will surely do exploits and be known as a leader in any field of endeavor.

If you want to know if you are mentally free, check your decisions and the impact that other people have over your mind. Then, if you are not satisfied with your findings, take on Reiki. After the session, you will testify to the fact that there is something known as mental freedom.

Don't shut your mind off from the help it needs; let Reiki step in and make a difference. As you learn to rely on Reiki for these small things, you will learn how to trust the process when dealing with huge issues entirely.

The state of your mind determines the state of your life, so choose freedom today by sticking to the universal energy for a reformed mental state. Whatever you do will always be a reflection of your mental freedom or otherwise. With Reiki, you have an opportunity to experience mental freedom for a long time.

Assists the Body in Eliminating Toxins

Reiki plays a very active role in supporting the body's immune system by cleaning out toxins. Through Reiki, our bodies are reminded to shift into the parasympathetic nervous system's self-healing mode.

Resting doesn't mean that you have to stop working or doing the things you love. It just means that your body will be signaled to sleep and digest better, which is crucial for the maintenance of health and vitality. The more time you spend in the Reiki space, the more active and productive you will be without feeling stressed out, having burn-outs, or getting exhausted.

If there are toxins in your body that builds up gradually, there is a higher chance that you wouldn't know until it becomes too late and you break down with an ailment. So, Reiki spots those toxins and helps it get rid of them before they constitute a bigger problem for you.

With toxins gone, your body will not experience imbalances anymore, and you can rest easy knowing that a major cause of illness has been defeated.

Promotes Natural Balance Between Mind, Body, and Spirit

A significant reason why you go through some days feeling less accomplished even though you put in so much effort is that there is a lack of harmony between the three most important aspects of your life, such as your body, mind, and spirit.

Sometimes your mind tells you to do something, and you find yourself doing something else, which leads to unrest within your spirit. With regular Reiki treatment, you can achieve greater harmony with these three elements such that you also strike a natural between them.

Mental balance enhances learning, mental clarity, and memory. It helps an individual cope with stress and alleviates mood swings. When your energies are correctly positioned, you will find that there are no confusions in your life.

All your decisions (mental, physical, and spiritual) will be in sync because they are all in alignment. This also means that your relationships will be purposeful, and you will be able to deal wisely with everyone else. We should all strive for balance in life. However, more importantly, we should aim to attain it in the long run.

Reiki helps you achieve balance and enables you to stick to it by empowering your mind to always to be attuned with your spirit and your body. This way, you wouldn't feel like you are doing anything contradictory the next time you make a decision. Your life will be like a natural flowing stream with no waves and complete calm as events unfold.

With Reiki, you can also stay centered in the present moment instead of getting caught up in the regrets and mistakes of the past. You will even notice if you have a harmonious reaction to people. For example, it is possible that in the past you told someone that you accept their apology, but in your mind, you are still upset about what they did.

When you use Reiki long enough, as you tell the person you have accepted his or her apology, it will be the same thing in your mind and spirit. There will be no grudges or hidden bitterness, thus helping you become a better person.

Reduces Depression and Anxiety

Reiki is very instrumental in aiding changes with your mood. The root causes of depression and anxiety are negative moods that rub off on everything else about you. With Reiki, you tend to feel better and more positive because you are receiving life force energy that dissolves energetic blockages.

It is difficult for a person who is continuously exposed to life force energy to become depressed or anxious. Once you come in contact with this energy form, your life gets better. No one is saying that you wouldn't have challenges, but even with them, you will be able to overcome them, thus avoiding being depressed or anxious.

In addition to a significant reduction with anxious and depressed feelings, you will also observe that you no longer give room for anger in your life. All of them (depression, violence, and anxiety) are negative expressions of being dissatisfied with life.

However, with Reiki, there are no negativities, which means that universal energy is the best form of treatment that you need to fight off depression and anxiety. Reiki works by helping you boost your mood because, when you have improved moods, anxiety tends to wear out, and you look at the world with the eyes of positivity.

Depression leads to a loss of vigor and excitement to do the things that you love, but you can regain all of that after a Reiki session(s). Remember that Reiki permeates all aspects of your body and its general composition, including the material and non-material ones.

So, when you go for Reiki session, you should tell the healer that you are dealing with depression and get it out of your system for good. However, what happens after the session? What if I start to feel anxious afterwards? There are fewer chances of you going back to that path again after getting healed because the meeting balances your chakra and resets the root causes of the problem in your mind.

Do not think about getting depressed again. Focus on enjoying your new mental freedom, and you will be able to sustain it. We will discuss sustainability in the next chapter, so look out for that section.

Eases Pain

There are several reasons for pain in the body, but one thing we can all agree on is the fact that it isn't pleasant. From shoulder to wrist pain, back pain, etc. working hours, age, and sleeping or sitting positions can be responsible for pain in the body.

While you are advised to make corrections with some of these cases, you can use universal energy to reverse the impact of the pain in your body. Reiki is about motion. The energy is always in motion, while pain represents something that is stuck somewhere in the body.

So, when universal energy sets in, it flows through your body and gets those stuck energies and blockages out, thus causing immediate or gradual relief to your body. However, listen to this, if you go back to the activities and things that cause you to feel the pain, you will be creating a vicious circle for yourself. The Reiki healer will probably tell you this, too.

Get your healing and go back to the office to make changes on the chair that isn't good for your back, join a gym, or become active with exercises that will keep pain at bay. Yes, Reiki can help, but you have to do better with things you can avoid. Once you use Reiki to take care of yourself with regards pain, make sure that your health is your priority, and you are proactive with maintaining the results that you have gotten with Reiki.

Reduces Stress

Stress reduction is one of the most popular benefits of Reiki. Even if you have booked a session for something else, one thing is for sure: you would come back feeling less stressed out in addition to the benefits you booked the session for.

Most sicknesses and diseases today are linked to stress. There's environmental anxiety, emotional stress, work-related stress, or even self-induced stress. All of these patterns will lead to irregular heartbeat, eating disorders, mood swings, and even sexual problems.

So, most of the time, a person carries the weight of being stressed on his or her shoulders. However, when they show up for a Reiki session, and the healer places his or her hands on their shoulders, they can feel the stress slowly ebb away.

Universal energy can trigger a more satisfying feeling within you that makes it possible for you to concentrate on what you can do instead of taking on too much at a time. More importantly, you will intentionally stay off anything that will induce stress after the Reiki session because your body has gotten a glimpse into how life can be without feeling stressed all the time.

Universal energy has the potential to help you redefine your life and become a protector of your mind space, in the sense that the decisions you make are not solely influenced by what you can do for others (which puts you under a lot of pressure) but based on what you can satisfactorily and with peace of mind.

It is safe to say that aside from the benefits you get from Reiki sessions, you are also passively taught how to treat yourself and make better decisions. You are encouraged to take care of your mental space because, if anything goes wrong in there, something can go wrong anywhere else.

Heals Infection and Inflammation

There are some treatments or surgeries that a person goes through that leads to inflammation in the body or infection without the person even realizing it. Some people will say that they feel weak with abnormal body temperature. They try to get treated for it without realizing that it is the fault of the inflammation or infection.

If you had surgery recently or just got cured of a disease or ailment, pay attention to how you feel for the next couple of days. If you don't feel great even after taking drugs, try Reiki.

Sometimes the healing that comes from Reiki when dealing with inflammation or infection may seem like a miracle because it is often instant. You can live an infection free life every day. It isn't an assumption but a possibility. Still, first, you know what to do and stick to it.

Reiki isn't just an option for ailments. When inflammation and infections are not well taken care of, then it can lead to severe illnesses. So, using Reiki against the disease shouldn't be done after a health scare but as a preventive measure to keep the body in check at all times.

When Reiki therapy is administered, you will find that you are relieved of the anxiety and worry that these issues may have caused you. The more focused you are on getting more universal energy, the more your body builds the resistance against inflammation and infection.

When we say Reiki helps you maintain good health or keeps you healthy, this is an example of how it works because a person who is free from infection and inflammation long-term is on the path to sustainable health.

Helps You Feel Empowered

The reason a lot of people struggle with the feeling of empowerment is that they are never calm enough to get to know who they are and accept themselves that way. The busier they are, the more distant they become, and this makes them feel empowered.

Reiki has a potent and calming effect. You will always feel calm in your sessions, and when you are in that calm state, you experience the freedom to accept your flaws and embrace the good qualities you embody.

This also means you become aware of the character traits you need to work on. As you work on them, you feel empowered because, unlike in the past, no one can use these flaws against you anymore. Hopelessness also goes away when universal energy is introduced. A recipient once said that after the session, he felt like a brand-new man, and this is the reason why he feels empowered as well.

Empowerment gives you the ability to take charge of your life by steering it in the direction that you want. To be more explicit, the power will be in your hands. With everything you've learned thus far, you know that the hands are very potent with universal energy.

Even when you are not in a Reiki session with a healer, you can practice it on yourself to create a lasting impact. You can always rely on it whenever you feel less empowered. Take advantage of the calming effect that Reiki offers by being fully immersed in every session so that there can be a deep fellowship with yourself and the universal energy.

So many things can be corrected in your life when you feel empowered and not defeated. Reiki is the way to go in bringing that feeling of empowerment to your consciousness.

Increases Creative Juices

If you have always struggled with being innovative, it isn't because you were born that way but because you are consciously or unconsciously blocking off the creative energy. A significant thing that happens in people's lives and is responsible for the lack of creative juices is stress.

Reiki can help you reduce or completely eradicate your stress levels while aiding clarity and focus. When you have not stressed out anymore, and your mind is to streamline to capture new ideas, then you can say your creative juices are back.

Reiki breaks down energetic blocks, and once you are free of these blocks, you tend to find new avenues and inspiration to generate ideas using your imaginative ability. The truth is that the ability has always been there; you didn't acknowledge it because you weren't even conscious of it in the first place.

After a Reiki session, go back to those things you found too difficult to do. Go back to those tasks you needed ideas on and try to get them done. You will observe that there are no more mental restrictions or difficulties because whatever was constituting a mental blockage has been taken care of by Reiki.

Remember that we have mentioned that universal energy does so much more than it's intended for in a given session because it is energy that flows through your body and fixes whatever needs to be fixed. If your challenge is with the creative juices that you need for your job, business, or family, then you can rest easy knowing that universal energy will take care of it for you.

Now, don't try to force the creative juices after a Reiki session. Relax and let it flow; don't doubt or wonder if it will happen because thoughts like that can affect you negatively.

Helps You Magnetize Abundance

Have you ever heard the statement, "You are a product of what you think about the most"? If you had, and you think back to the events in your life, then you will agree that the things you give so much attention to through your thoughts will often manifest. The universe uses a very fair method to present what you desire through your will. If you think you deserve to be happy, then happiness is what you get from the universe.

The same principle applies to everything else in life, from prosperity to abundance. Everything good you desire can come to you just by channeling the right energy, and Reiki is the conduit that you need to tap into to gain the universe's positive energy.

When you show up for a Reiki session, you do not only get to feel the hands of the healed but also learn how to be much more affirmative by using the energy generated through Reiki to touch the things around you. You can see an energy-charged ball transform whatever you want and make it suit your life entirely.

The more you are in contact with the vibration that brings more abundance to people's lives, the more you can attract it into your life. This is why consistent Reiki sessions are always advised. Now, no one is saying that you should show up at the healer's place every day or demand distant healing daily.

You can schedule the sessions to be just about the right amount of time you will need to get the energy for abundance and then magnetize it through self-Reiki sessions.

Creating a comprehensive book like this one takes a lot of effort because of the amount of research required, and we have genuinely achieved so much with the chapters and sections thus far. It is time to wrap up the journey on a very inspiring note.

The next chapter will take you through the process of sustainability with all things Reiki. It will be the last chapter, an opportunity to inspire you to take action so that these benefits can become a palpable experience.

Chapter Six: The Concept of Continuity with Reiki

Do you know why Christmas is always a magical experience for kids? It is because of the continuing tradition with Christmas gifts, Santa Clause, holiday cheer, and every other thing that makes the season special. So, a child goes through this process from a tender age till he or she becomes a teenager and will always remember the magic of Christmas.

Now, Reiki isn't a seasonal experience like Christmas, but it can completely transform your life in a wholesome way. So, why not think about sustaining this feeling?

Some people discover the excitement of Reiki, bask in the feeling for a few days, and forget about the experience. Others, however, do not forget intentionally but say, "Life happens." This is why they must take an intentional approach towards ensuring that they sustain and continue the healing process.

More often than not, when there is a discourse on universal energy and treatment options, there is very little attention to how people can sustain what they learn and keep up with their sessions.

Nothing good will last long if there is no effort to ensure its continuity. You want to make sure that this fantastic experience you have going for yourself continues and that you are inspired to do more with Reiki other than simply know how it works.

This chapter will introduce you to some ideas that will ensure the continuity of your Reiki experience. It is the perfect way to bring this journey to an end.

Note: The steps you will find below cut across what both healers and recipients can do to sustain the practice. So, depending on what you are going after, there is an idea for both sides of the treatment option.

How to Sustain Reiki in Your life

Show Up for Sessions

If you are very serious about sustainability with your Reiki practice and healing, then you must develop the discipline to show up for all your recommended meetings. There is a small group of people who believe that Reiki doesn't work and that it isn't as effective as the healers make it be. Such people speak from the incompetent experiences they had and will do whatever they can to make others believe them.

Well, the reason why they say that is because they didn't complete their sessions or stick to the advice or caution of the practitioners. While others have amazing Reiki stories to tell, they don't. If you don't show up for sessions, you will end up like such person.

It takes a lot of commitment to get the best out of Reiki. In some situations, one session is enough. For others, though, you will need more than one. Still, the decision isn't yours to make, especially if you aren't doing self-treatment. The healer will decide on that because he or she is the one who is handling the session and will know what you need.

If you aspire to become a professional healer someday, how do you intend to help your patients get better when you can't adhere to your own healer's advice? Reiki is never about convenience or a perfectly suited time or when you feel like doing it.

If you have a pressing challenge, and you are keen on taking care of it, you must be willing to do whatever is required to make it happen. We are not talking about achieving healing today and struggling with the same thing the next week; we are seeking ways through which you can become a walking testimony of the impact of Reiki and achieve that. Therefore, consistency with sessions is required.

Now I know that some individuals may have hectic schedules, even though they genuinely want to complete their sessions. If you are such a person, then you must learn how to prioritize and manage your time well enough so that you can do everything necessary.

Reiki practitioners are not just all about helping you with your ailment or psychological challenge. They are also humane individuals who are trained to understand the value of time. Instead of procrastinating your sessions or not showing up for them at all, reach out to your healer and explain your peculiar situation.

Let the healer know that you are willing to work around your schedule, but you need help. By doing this, you will be helping yourself as you take on so many things at once, which can lead to stress. Now, you want to ensure that you can sustain the Reiki impact. If you don't know how to manage it with your schedule, speak to your healer.

It wouldn't be nice if, after reading this book, you end up like some people who say that Reiki doesn't work because you didn't commit to the process entirely. We have not only been on a journey together with this book, but you have also invested in your life by purchasing it. So, how do you get the dividends of the investment?

You achieve the latter by being committed to the process and ensuring that you give it your best at all times. You can sustain the Reiki impact. Start by not missing out on sessions, and you will be amazed at the level of progress you make with your experience long-term.

Be Attentive to Your Body

Another step that you can take towards sustaining Reiki is being attentive to your body. Reiki is all about energy, and energy is about awareness. In fact, if you are not someone who is easily attuned or discerning of energy around yourself, you surely cannot get the benefits of Reiki long-term.

Meaning, if you are not someone who pays close attention to these things, you will need more practice, and the best way to do that is by listening to your body.

Your body speaks to you all the time. The question is, are you listening? Are you paying attention to the signs and signals that it's sending to you? Some people go for a Reiki session; because they are not attentive to their bodies, though, they don't know what takes place in it. They don't know if they have been healed; they cannot feel the energy permeate their bodies. For this reason, they can never succeed with the idea of sustainability as well.

After ensuring that you have not skipped even one session, you should pay close attention to what your body is trying to say to you. That is the only way you can ascertain the extent of healing you've received and anything else.

Below, you will discover a step that advises you to share your experience with others and help them, but how do you intend sharing with them when you don't know what happened to you? When you are sharing your story with people, and they ask questions regarding the impact of Reiki on your body, what will you say? If you haven't been listening to your body, today is an excellent time to start.

Shut out the noise around you for a few minutes every day. Some people call it meditation, but this time you will seek to listen to your voice. When you shut out everything, wait for a few minutes. With your mind's eye, roam around your body and listen to your heartbeat. Does it seem regular to you? Do you feel tired? Is your body saying something through your new sleep duration?

I am so keen on helping you listen to your body because a lot of ailments and problems that people seek Reiki for are preventable if they have paid attention to their bodies. So, in those moments when you listen, if there is something amiss, share it with your healer or practice Reiki on yourself using the hand movements you've been taught earlier.

Over time, you will find that you don't need to run to the hospital every time there is a little health scare because your body communicates with you, and you listen to it. The universal energy that you get through Reiki will also keep your body stable, so you are always healthy, optimistic, and excited about life.

Learn More

It doesn't matter what you think you already know. There is always more to learn, especially if you want to be a Reiki healer or practitioner for a long while. The most successful therapists do not stop learning. In fact, they intentionally study every day because they realize that nothing will stay the same all year long.

If you don't make attempts to learn and discover more about Reiki, you will become obsolete. Hence, you will no longer be as effective as you used to be. As recipients feel like they are not getting help from you, they will seek other Reiki healers, and you will lose clients.

Building a good reputation as a healer is part of the process. You don't become a reputable one all of a sudden. It takes a lot of work, which lies within your ability to make the sessions work.

Don't stop learning Reiki with this book. Read more materials, listen to successful practitioners, attend seminars and workshops, register for personal coaching lessons, and even do some on-the-job training to know what it's like to work with recipients. If you are committed to the idea of sustainability, then it means you want to practice for a long time. For that to happen, you must be committed to continuing and vigorously learning new procedures.

Think about doctors, lawyers, and people in other professions. It takes them quite a while to become professionals; they go through years of training at varying levels of difficulty as well. You are dealing with the idea that will liberate a lot of individuals from their challenges, and you are attuned to the universe. For this reason, you must take your profession seriously as well.

In the olden days when Reiki just became popular, it wasn't so easy for people who desired to become healers to get further training. Some even had to travel to learn from masters. These days, though, technology has made it easier for anyone who is willing to gain knowledge about Reiki.

Meanwhile, if you don't have money to pay for the more exclusive trainings, you can start with the free ones from blogs. There are also online platforms that are solely dedicated to Reiki training. Before adopting any of the approaches you see virtually, make sure that the website is verified and that you are getting authentic content that suits your desire for success with Reiki.

The more you learn and practice, the better you become, and then you can advance to higher heights with your Reiki practice. You wouldn't learn everything within a specified time frame, so I cannot tell you that it will take one or two years. Several doctors with years of experience still get to learn new facts about their profession every day, after all. If you are keen on being the best in this field, therefore, you must be willing to become aggressive and committed to learning.

Don't Be Selfish

This step is so important, and we cannot bring this book to a close without talking about it. If you are practicing or intend to practice Reiki selfishly with the sole aim of making money, you will be causing a lot of harm to your reputation and the field in general.

Do not practice Reiki just because you want to profit from clients or gain control and prestige. You will have a stubborn time proving your expertise if you do that. Also, Reiki isn't about you, your selfish motives, or what you will derive from it.

Reiki is all about the person who is healed, as well as the role of the healer in connecting the life force energy to the recipient. What's most striking is the fact that you will not be able to establish a thriving practice because you would struggle with gaining access to guidance from the spirit.

If your connection to the universal energy doesn't have a strong spiritual base, then you cannot tap into the universe's energy quickly. A motive is significant since, as a healer, you will be the conduit for the healing the recipient will receive. What kind of channel you want to be, a selfish one who only thinks about themselves? Alternatively, do you want to become a selfless channel?

You must get to know what your motives are before taking the next step towards practicing Reiki. Don't decide on becoming an expert because it seems like a good title or business idea. You must look beyond yourself and what you will gain and continually strive to seek the greater good of all men and women who may cross your path.

If you have read through this book, and you feel that stirring sensation within you to make a difference in the world, then it means that Reiki is for you. When you pursue it, you can be sure of gaining success in this field. On the contrary, if all you see is a business opportunity, I will advise you not to take any step further towards becoming a Reiki practitioner now.

Spread the Word, Help Others

Sustainability will not be possible without the people who want to try out Reiki. So, if you are not concerned about anyone else but yourself, why are you reading this book? It is essential for everyone who wants to practice Reiki, as well as the ones who benefit from it, to take a step forward by reaching out to others.

Think about this for a second. If the earliest practitioners didn't try to help other people, would we ever know about Reiki today? You see, this step has been in use for years now because it is the one thing that guarantees sustainability.

This book and several others in this niche were written by seasoned authors who want to contribute their know-how to the sustainability movement by keeping the topic alive within most human interactions. Hence, if you have a successful Reiki story, why aren't you sharing it?

People only believe what they know can happen. We trust medicines, hospitals, and doctors because we have been taking drugs since we were kids and getting cured of illnesses. However, imagine if a doctor comes forward and says something can work, but he or she doesn't have any proof. Will you believe this physician and take a chance?

Theoretical knowledge doesn't inspire people. After all, anyone can write anything they want. Nevertheless, when individuals hear your distinct story when they know that this thing can transform their lives for good in ways they can only imagine, they will be willing to take a step towards it.

There are two ideas that are related to sustainability. The first one is the concept of spreading the word, and the second one is the concept of helping others. You cannot do one and leave the other. As you take steps towards spreading the word about Reiki, to be specific, you will have to reach out to help others as well.

Now, you don't have to take on an entire neighborhood or a bunch of people at the same time. Sart with your closest friends and family members who may be dealing with one health challenge or another. Introduce them to Reiki and then explain in detail what Reiki is about. If they have questions, try to provide answers but do not exaggerate anything so that they will not have to hold on to unrealistic expectations. If they are keen on books, you can share this book with them.

Considering your loved ones are excited about Reiki enough to want to give it a try, then you can use the second approach, which entails helping others. You try a Reiki treatment session on them to help with their challenge. If you have been self-treating yourself, and you haven't healed someone else before, it may feel strange to you at first. Still, there's no need to worry because we know that you can do this!

Just ensure that you have practiced on yourself long enough and that you have achieved results before helping someone else. Doing self-treatment and treating others are the same. Only, with the latter, you will be channeling the universal energy into someone else's body.

Even if you have a friend who is far away, you can use the distant healing techniques you were taught earlier to make it happen. The point is that, by reaching out to others who need help, you will not only be contributing positively to someone else's life, but you will also be advancing your skills and getting better every day.

Take some time off to practice so that you can feel confident about what you are doing. Sustainability is all about carrying on with the tradition we gained (as others did before us). It is your contribution to the Reiki story. Although it may not be a story that is told globally, in your little way, you will be adding value to the lives of others.

There is more to say and achieve with Reiki, so take time to dig in through research. As you learn more, you will become empowered to share with the world what you have gained. Most healers are inspired by their desire to make the world a better place, to be honest. They see their gift not as a skill but as a medium through which they can contribute positively to the well-being of others.

Experience and Heart (Passion)

If you want to be a successful Reiki practitioner, it is crucial that you become conscious of the concept of experience and heart.

A lot of times, when people discover what they love and what they want to do, they often stick to the books and materials that instruct them how to garner experience. Others take on the job so seriously because they want to be at the top of the game. Well, it is significant to be concerned about the experience, but what about passion?

No one is hugely successful at whatever they do without being passionate about it. For sustainability to become effective with your practice, therefore, there must be room for passion in yourself.

Passion keeps a practitioner going even when it seems like he or she is dealing with daunting challenges.

Make no mistake about this; the experience can never replace passion, regardless of how experienced you are. It is possible that you will throw in the towel and give up sooner than later because you lack passion. Passion is that feeling of excitement you have within you that helps you navigate through the process of helping others with ease.

Some people are highly paid in their jobs, for instance. They have this fantastic office and everything else going for them. However, it turns out that they despise their position. Yes, they enjoy the perks the job brings, but they always think about how different their lives would have been if they could do something they love. Similarly, the bank executive with a cool ride and a driver may be thinking about the passion that he or she has for baking.

Life can be funny like this sometimes. You have an opportunity right now to make this Reiki practice work. This way, you don't end up feeling like you have made a mistake later on. By making it work, I mean building experience and passion at the same time.

First, you become passionate about something by making sure that this is what you want to do. Then, you start practicing it. However, you don't stop working on your passion every day. The best way to keep your determination burning is by going over and beyond everyone else to do the most as a Reiki practitioner.

Show up every day at your workspace with so much glee and excitement like you haven't been doing this for a while, for instance. Don't get too comfortable or too familiar with the process as well. Otherwise, it will become like a regular job. Remember, people are not passionate about regular jobs!

The combination of passion and experience is unbeatable. You will watch yourself rise like an edifice in this field. You will become even more productive with your recipients as there will be a lot of success stories from your sessions. Still, you must provide an answer to the all-important question, "Do I want to be a Reiki healer?"

Don't rush off to answer this one. Take some time to think about it with all the information you have received so far. Try to think objectively without emotional affiliations or any pressure.

Being a Reiki practitioner is excellent but being a passionate one who is poised to garner more experience is exceptionally perfect!

We used a mini portion of this book to discuss the history of Reiki and mentioned some of the individuals in the past who did well with it. Well, those people are still talked about today in Reiki circles because they weren't just experienced but also passionate about what they did to help others. That feeling, combined with experience, made them great in this field. You can enjoy the same process as well if you try to discover what you are passionate about and how you can build your Reiki experience.

When you get a job for the first time in a firm that you love so much, for instance, from your first day at work, you already start to strategize regarding how you are going to get promoted to the top and get a corner office. The reason why you have such ambition is that you don't want to be stagnant in life.

Work With an Illumined Being

Another way through which you can improve your effectiveness with Reiki is by developing a working relationship with an illumined being. Yes, there are Reiki guides who help us with our sessions, but they may not be able to provide you with the highest form of help available. So, you will need to develop a working relationship with an illumined being.

This illumined being gets its energy directly from the source, God, the universe, the Supreme Being, or whatever you choose to call it. The illumined being is not egotistic and offers a pure form of guidance as they possess extraordinary skills. Their energy is refined, and they can interact with you in a myriad of ways that are suited for you in particular.

The energies they use can be adjusted, and healing will happen in the most efficient manner. More importantly, the illumined individual will always respect your free will and get permission from you before providing any help regardless of what you want. Whether your goal is to improve your Reiki skills or upgrade your healing energy, for instance, the illumined being can help you attain them. If you are already working with a guide, the illumined being can also work closely with them by enabling an upgrade of their skills and improving the quality of their healing energy.

Now, the illumined beings have different names depending on the religious context or the spiritual background of the person seeking their help. Some people call them Jesus; others say that it is Mother Mary, the Holy Spirit, Krishna, Buddha, the Archangels, etc. You may already be utilizing your relationship with any of these illumined beings, but if you don't know how to be in touch with them, the steps below will serve as a guide.

How to Get Help from an Illumined Being

Say a prayer or affirmation

First, you begin by saying a prayer or statement, asking for guidance from the illumined being. This is the first step that you must take after deciding on the illumined nature that you want to work with.

The prayer and affirmation will be the start of the relationship with the illumined being. That will also give you an opportunity to get comfortable with their presence.

Set a time to meditate

You will need to set a particular time during the day that is suitable for meditation. Your times of reflection will help you stay attuned with the illumined being and get used to the unique energy that comes with it.

Pray to the illumined being

At the start of your meditation, pray to the illumined being you have decided to work with so that he or she can make contact with you and strengthen the connection. While praying, you ought to specifically mention the reason why you are reaching out and why you need guidance.

Tell the illumined being that you are passionate about helping others, but you need help in making that happen. At this stage, you should be as open as you can be because every other aspect of this connection will be hinged on what you say in your prayer.

Use the Reiki distance symbol

Next, use the Reiki distance symbol by sending your energy to the illumined being. As you do this, continue with prayers and affirmations; ask the being to work through you and strengthen your energy or connections.

Pray for the illumined being to also enhance your universal energy so that it can be much more effective and beneficial to the individuals you use it on.

Ask for guidance

Ask the illumined being to become your main guide and the main source of your energy. Then, give them permission to heal and make changes within your energy field as it deems fit for your healing.

Right now, you need guidance because others will be coming to you for it. With the illumined being working through you, there is hope of getting support and advice that will enable you to practice Reiki more effectively.

Ask for support

If you are working with guides already, now will also be a good time to ask the illumined body to support and work with them in upgrading their skills and healing energies. You can ask whatever you want in line with Reiki practice, so always feel free to do so in that meditative state.

Remove unhealthy spirits

During the session, you can ask the illumined being to help you get rid of harmful spirits or any other forces that may not be a part of God's plan for you. Now, it is possible that there are negative energies present in your life that affects your Reiki services to recipients.

Ask the illumined being to get the false energies out of your space or environment, too, so that you can practice freely without unnecessary interferences from the wrong vibration.

Use your free will

Illumined beings do not try to exert their will on you; they will always respect your wishes and free will by not forcing anything on you. They will ask permission before making changes with the energy field or providing healing.

Take advantage of this free will and ask for anything else you would like to happen to you or through your Reiki practice. When you make such requests in line with wanting to do good for others, the illumined being will most likely grant your request.

Be guided with your hands

While still in session with the illumined being, place your hands on different parts of your body so that you can appropriate healing there and allow the illumined being's energy to flow through you.

If you have problematic areas or health challenges while praying, use your hands to create contact between your body and the energy from the illumined being. In some cases, you will receive direction on the parts of your body that you should touch, so you should pay attention to what you are doing at all times.

End with a prayer of gratitude

All your sessions with the illumined being should end with a prayer of gratitude and with a request for them to continue helping, guiding, and supporting you with their blessings. You are going to help several other people get better as well, so now is the time to ask for protection from the illumined being and stay grateful for the prayers that you believe are already answered.

You can do this illumined being meditation once daily or as your schedule will allow. It will give you a chance to contemplate this great desire you feel to help others and make the world a better place with Reiki. Remember that this is a very powerful exercise. If you do it continually for a period of years, it will become a huge part of your life.

The illumined being has boundless potentials that can heal you and empower you to do the same for others. Soon enough, they become your only guide (with God, of course). This will quicken your spiritual path while helping your work to get better and better like never before.

It may seem like a process with a lot of steps, but the truth is that if you can get it right within the first few weeks, it will become a part of you long-term. There is so much potential for growth, increased well-being and healing. Still, for you to tap into that potential, you must reach out to a higher authority that can help you create a spiritual pattern.

You cannot succeed with sustaining Reiki if you don't have access to an illumined being. It's like having access to God directly. What can be more potent than that?

Now that you have access to the fundamental aspects of Reiki, always think about getting better and doing better. Look beyond how well you may be doing now and realize that you can do even more if you are dedicated to the process.

The continuation of Reiki is a miracle. It unlocks several doors for you and keeps you inspired. Don't get excited about it once and forget about how well it can affect your life positively later. Just like those kids in Christmas Morning, allow the magic of Reiki to work through you for self-healing and helping others as well.

Well, with this chapter, we can say that we are at the end of our journey, and it has been an exciting one. I believe that you have learned so much about Reiki and that you are ready to implement everything that you know at this point. Concerning implementation, there is a concluding section that you must read as it contains a call to action that will inspire you to utilize the information you have just gained.

Conclusion

Reiki has been used in various forms, and if it has had a long and fruitful history, then it is worth a try. Life will always come at you with varying issues, from the ones you expect to the ones you didn't see coming. Despite the emotional and personal challenges, it is possible for you to overcome them in the most natural way, which is also safe.

Reiki has transcended the level of skepticism and assumptions. We are dealing with a very important healing process that can completely transform your life for good. Hence, in the sections and chapters above, you received extensive details about how to utilize Reiki, as well as other vital information that would make it work for you.

Every human being starts to become concerned about his or her well-being from an early stage in life but being worried about how you feel or the events that cause you to experience imbalanced emotions isn't enough. You must intentionally seek ways to get solutions. That is where Reiki comes into the picture.

In addition to the chapters on ailments and benefits of Reiki, you should also know that Reiki gives a positive boost to your mental health. The #1 topic out there on the internet and everywhere else is the impact of mental health.

If you are wondering why this is the case in 2019, you don't have to anymore because technological disruption enabled a lot of innovations of which social media is at its peak. There are so many people who are completely enthralled by their mobile phones, social media accounts, and the concept of living to impress other people who don't even care about them.

The more involved they are with this circle, the less attention they pay to their mental health, which ultimately leads to a breakdown that could have been avoided. With techniques such as Reiki, one will agree that concerns about mental health can be laid to rest as the well-being of the individual becomes the focus of attention.

Before putting this book down, commit to utilizing Reiki as a self-help practice of protecting your mental health and well-being. It is easier to read a book than implement the details it expresses; this is what separates the people who live well from the one who do not. The former takes action on knowledge gained while the latter does nothing about it.

Remember that Reiki is not an alternative treatment for medical challenges but adjunctive therapeutic support for healing and boosting someone's well-being. If you can get it right with Reiki, then you can get it right with a lot of things mentally, emotionally, and physically.

References

Contessa, L. (2018). 16 Basic Hand position for Self Reiki. Retrieved from https://medium.com/@contessalouise/16-basic-hand-positions-for-self-reiki-c7e19ed6b3f6

Dave, N. (2017). Lifeforce Energy Optimization: How to Experience Transformational Healing. Retrieved from https://www.reikiinfinitehealer.com/lifeforce-energy-optimization

David, H. (2015). Traditional hand positions for Reiki Treatment. Retrieved from https://thereikipage.com/handpos.html

International Association of Reiki Professionals. (2019). Learn about Reiki. Retrieved from https://iarp.org/history-of-reiki/

Indianetzone Reiki, Diseases Cured by Reiki. (n.d.). Retrieved from https://health.indianetzone.com/reiki/1/diseases_cured_by_reiki.htm

Kathie, L. (n.d.). Distant Healing and the Human Energy Field. Retrieved from https://www.reiki.org/reikinews/distanthealing.htm

Palmer, Miles/ (2011), How to Practice Reiki Self-Treatments. Retrieved from https://reikiinmedicine.org/daily-practice/how-to-practice-reiki-self-treatment/

The Thirsty Soul, Benefits of Reiki. (n.d.) Retrieved from, https://www.thethirstysoul.com/reiki/benefits-of-reiki/

University of Minnesota, What can I Expect in a Typical Reiki Session? (n.d.) Retrieved from https://www.takingcharge.csh.umn.edu/what-can-i-expect-typical-reiki-session

Guided Mindfulness Meditation

How to overcome negativity and anxiety in your daily life with the practice of mindfulness.

Caroline Kirkman

Introduction

Congratulations on purchasing this book and thank you for doing so. This book will help you in understanding the concept of Mindfulness Meditation and would also walk you through the whole process with its guided meditations.

Mindfulness meditation is a way to raise consciousness levels and improve control over emotions and reactions. Out of all the meditation techniques popular these days, mindfulness is the easiest to implement in the modern lifestyle. It is a practical way to bring a thorough change in your life.

These days meditation has become a highly popular technique to solve the mysteries of the mind. However, meditation is simply a tool. You can practice it for brief periods in a day and hence the results are limited.

Mindfulness meditation is a way of life. Through meditation, you can unravel the mysteries of your mind and mindfulness becomes a way of life which can significantly improve your quality of life.

This book will help you in understanding the overall concept of mindfulness in detail and the ways in which you can incorporate it into your life. This book will explain in detail all the concepts related to the implementation of mindfulness in practical life.

This book has several guided meditations for not one but various mindfulness meditation techniques to make implementation easy for you.

It also has guided meditations for simple processes like breathing and relaxing to complex issues like anxiety and panic relief.

Great emphasis has been given to explain all the aspects of mindfulness meditation so that you face no difficulty in giving it a sincere try.

In this book, on one hand, you will get information about the basic but crucial concepts like posture, techniques, and building focus. On the other hand, you will get to understand the ways to cultivate important tenants like acceptability, forgiveness, gratefulness, etc.

From extensive breathing exercises to comprehensive guided meditations, this book is your complete guide to mindfulness meditation.

Every effort has been made to ensure that this book delivers complete and comprehensive information about meditation to you. I hope that you will find it highly informative and useful.

There are plenty of books on this subject on the market, thanks again for choosing this one! Every effort was made to ensure it is full of as much useful information as possible, please enjoy!

Chapter 1: What is Mindfulness?

Mindfulness and Its Importance in Bringing down Stress, Anxiety, and Panic Attacks

Mindfulness is the quality of being aware or conscious. It may not sound much but most of our actions are not conscious decisions. We don't act, we react. One action leads to another action and then we get bound in the act of reacting. Our actions become mechanical. Many of our actions are simply a copy of the trends. Even our impulsive or spontaneous decisions are also influenced by peer pressure or any other kind of pressure. This means that most of the actions that we take in our day to day lives are not conscious decisions. They are reactionary decisions.

Mindfulness is the ability to develop the consciousness to make deliberate decisions. It gives us the ability to act and not just to react.

The steep increase in the stress levels in the people is a testimony that we have surrendered the control of our lives to others. What's even more dangerous, we have surrendered to our subconscious mind which runs on recorded memory. It is reactive and not proactive.

People suffering from panic attacks and anxiety disorders are so common that it has started to look scary. All this isn't happening due to external factors but because we have started paying less importance to crucial things. We are trying to do symptomatic and superficial treatments of everything. We fail to address the core issues and without that, the problems would remain as they were.

Before we move ahead, I'd like to tell a small story.

Once there lived an old man Frank

One day the jolly natured frank was frantically looking for something in his yard. His neighbor John noticed this and came to the help of Frank. He came to know that Frank was looking for his car keys. John also started the search and both of them looked in the whole yard for the key in vain. Tired and exasperated John asked the old man if he remembered anything about where he might have placed the keys last. Frank quipped he remembered placing them inside the home.

John was furious and failed to understand the level of stupidity of this octogenarian who was looking for the keys outside while he had placed them inside.

Yet, he controlled his emotions and simply asked the old man the reason for looking for the keys outside when he clearly remembers placing them inside. Frank simply replied, because the light outside was good.

This might look like a stupid reply but it is a reality of this age. We all are trying to heal the wounds of our feet by placing the ointment on our stomach.

We keep blaming others for our stress, anxiety, and anger. However, we forget that it is our mind which is leading to these emotions. All these are reactions and not actions. Someone else could have been hurtful, vindictive, abusive, conniving, and deceptive but the onus of keep getting hurt from those actions time and again is always on us.

Mindfulness is the way to understand the way our thought process functions and it is the tool to stop it from becoming reactionary.

Mindfulness can help you in gaining control of your thought process. It can help you in reacting to everything and harboring the wounds.

Newton's 3rd law of motion states that every action has an equal and opposite reaction. Every action that we take generates a reaction. However, that reaction then again leads to another reaction. A vicious chain of actions and reactions start.

If you are mindful, you will be able to understand the futility of reaction in the first place. You would be able to stop the generation of negativity. You'd get equipped to deal with your problems internally and hence wouldn't need revenge as a remedy.

What Makes It Different?

Mindfulness or Mindful movement is believed to have originated from the Buddhist insight meditation practices. It is the art of looking inwards. Although all forms of meditation seek to look inwards, this meditation is not trying to alter anything. It is simply striving to understand the cause of things.

The western emphasis has primarily been to bend the way our mind works. It has tried everything from pills to potions to manipulate the mind. It has been successful and unsuccessful at times. But, every attempt has had its impact.

The thing that makes mindfulness different from others is that it is simple to practice. It is easy to understand. It doesn't promise to provide solutions. It simply strives to provide answers.

It is not a way to get over the problems in life. The problems in life are a result of our actions. The only way to get over them is to take corrective steps. Mindfulness helps you in understanding the reason for those problems in your mind.

It is a way through which you can train your mind to become more conscious about decisions.

It can prevent you from becoming reactionary which is again a reason for most of our problems.

Being mindful doesn't mean that you wouldn't have feelings of anger, despair, or discontent. It simply means that you'll know the way to react so things don't escalate any further.

Above all, it can provide answers to most of your mind clutter. You can get a third-party view of your own mind from a premium location. It will help you in becoming more objective and reasonable.

Mindfulness and the Concept of Awareness

Being alive doesn't mean being aware. Awareness is a state of mind. It is a state in which you are conscious of everything. You stop making instinctive decisions. Your actions become balanced.

Mindfulness is a way of life in which you take even simple decisions with complete awareness. Your actions don't remain mechanical anymore. They get a sense of purpose and determination.

We are living in the most comfortable times ever. Humankind, as a race, has made tremendous progress.

- ✓ There is no fear of predators.
- ✓ We have greater food security.
- ✓ Bringing food to the table isn't a question of life and death anymore.
- ✓ Our dwellings are capable of providing much better protection against the ferocity of weather in most conditions.
- ✓ We have the luxury to keep our homes hot or cold irrespective of the weather outside.
- ✓ We have better means of treating diseases and have highly advanced medical facilities.
- ✓ The average human lifespan is also increasing gradually.

Just a few centuries ago, it could have been more than anything you could ask for.

Yet, we aren't happy with all this.

On the contrary, our lives are full of fear, anger, envy, stress, frustration, and a whole spectrum of such negative emotions.

These negative emotions bring unhappiness, sorrow, grief, and guilt into our lives. They weigh us down and negate our achievements.

They act like quicksand. We always feel trapped and things are pulling us further. We know we would never drown in them but getting out is also not that easy.

Getting out always looks like an easy possibility but most of us are never really able to get out of it. We end up spending our lives in a sorrowful, dejected, unsatisfied, and unhappy state.

It Wasn't Meant to Be like This

Initially, our ancestors started with the pursuit of happiness. They started the journey by addressing each and every issue that could bring happiness into their lives.

In the beginning, the empty belly was the biggest worry and hence food gave happiness. They learned better ways to get food to the table.

Then, the fear of enemies and predators became one of the biggest worries and hence they learned better ways to tackle both so that they could feel more secure and thus happy.

They learned to build better homes and boundaries for protection against intrusion and discomfort.

One after the other, they have gained victory over most of the things that could pose a question of life and death. They also learned the ways to accumulate things that could bring greater comfort and luxury.

However, in the process, our race got mixed up somewhere. Our quest to get better than the best and our lust to gain more and more prevailed over our pursuit of happiness. We started giving more importance to things that seemed to bring happiness rather than happiness itself. This has led to great confusion and also to most of the miseries that we are facing today.

Our mind has got fixated on things that seem to bring happiness. However, we don't have a clear definition of happiness. We have started looking for an abstract feeling in physical forms. This results in continuous failures. We keep running after things that have no significance in the greater scheme of things.

Most of the times these things lead to the cluttering of mind. The mind is always occupied with hundreds of thoughts. People are worried about the most inconsequential things like what are they going to have at dinner? The clothes they would like to buy? Did they lock the door properly? Did someone say something bad about them in the office behind their backs? What would the boss think of their actions? The list of such thoughts is endless.

It takes away all the calm and peace from life. These racing thoughts not only cause stress and anxiety, but they also bring doubt and self-pity. There remains no greater purpose for life. There is no long-term goal for life. Despite being a member of the most superior race on this planet, life starts to pass like all other creatures. We all have started living a life of consequences. Every action that we take is simply a reaction of action taken by others. There is no control or conscious thought.

This lack of control and compulsion of living a reactionary life clutters the mind even more. The mind is never at peace. It is always preparing strategies and counterstrategies. It is always busy. It always remains insecure. The more insecure it gets, the greater the negativity it builds around you as a protective shell. This can mess with lives in real terms.

Meditation is a way to get out of this quicksand of negative emotions. It gives you a chance to reclaim your life and energies. You are able to get hold of your mind and manage the incessant chatter inside it.

What Clutters the Mind

Modern life has become such that we all are suffering from information overload. There is a constant bombarding of data most of which is unsolicited. This creates clutter in mind. Our mind is constantly processing information which it doesn't even need.

Our lifestyles are such that we find ourselves in a constant decision-making dilemma. From choosing the shirt to wear for office to the things to have at lunch, we are constantly faced with the problem of making insignificant choices. These decisions may not look like much but they keep our mind engaged. All of us face the decision fatigue to a great extent and it has an effect on our decision making faculties and the ability of our brain to function efficiently. There is no surprise people are always so desperate to take breaks even though they are not really facing a very heavy workload in their personal and professional lives.

All these things are putting a lot of burden on our minds. The mind always remains under pressure of working constantly. It remains cluttered and becomes inefficient. There are so many decisions being taken in the background that it is always reeling under pressure. This also creates another problem and that is unconscious decision making.

We are living a life of consequences. Someone does something and all our actions are simply reactions to that action. We are constantly in a state of compulsive reaction. We have given the keys of our lives to others. A famous celebrity does something and you also want to do the same, without even thinking about the futility of the action. Someone abuses you on the way to work and the whole day your brain remains engaged thinking about it. Such things are reactions and not conscious actions.

This all happens when the mind is cluttered with unnecessary things and it gains so much power that eventually it starts to run you.

This is the condition which makes you compulsive, reactionary, and helpless.

This cluttering of mind can make life miserable. It takes away all the joy from life. It drives away the passion and spontaneity. Everything simply becomes a monotonous drill. The mind becomes the ruling authority.

Meditation is the way to declutter the mind. It helps you in observing your life from a distance for a moment so that you can make conscious decisions. If you want to achieve a state of thoughtless awareness where every decision is simply not a reaction to the actions in the past, meditation is the way to do that.

Advantages of Being Mindful

Scientific studies have conclusively proven that mindfulness can help in improving our cognitive behavior. It is an amazing way to increase happiness, contentment, patience, acceptance, gratitude, forgiveness and compassion in life.

Being mindful means that you wouldn't allow negative emotions like anger, frustration, and sadness to overcrowd your mind.

There can be a tremendous increase in your compassion levels and you may see a significant decrease in aggression. Your stress levels would go down considerably and you'd find it effortlessly easy to smile.

Some specific advantages of mindfulness meditation are:

Lowers Depression: This goes without saying that mindfulness can help in lowering depression. The major causes of depression lie layered in our subconscious. When our subconscious starts ruling our body, we have poor control over its powers. Mindfulness empowers you to look for answers that are hidden deep inside your mind. It tremendously helps in lowering depression.

Improved Ability to Control Mood and Anxiety: Anxiety and mood disorders are a result of a reactionary mechanism in our mind. We rely too much on the mental stimuli which are influenced by past instances. This leads to anxiety as your mind starts replaying or recreating past scenarios. You stop being proactive in life. Mindfulness helps in understanding the whole thought process that leads to the development of such ideas.

Help in Managing Stress: When you are conscious about your emotions, stressors, and triggers, you get an improved capability in managing stress levels. Your understanding of real problems in life improves.

Lowers Chances of Panic Attacks: Panic attacks take place when the train of thoughts gets out of control and your mind starts creating worst-case scenarios. This is mind going on an overdrive. Mindfulness can help in preventing this state to a great extent.

Lowers the Need for Substance Abuse: Substance abuse in most cases starts as a way to run away from problems that you can't handle. Mindfulness empowers you to handle all kinds of problems created by your mind. It enables you to face your worst fears. It eliminates the need for an artificial refuge.

Improved Focus: Mindfulness helps you in working on your awareness levels. Your concentration and ability to focus on things on purpose improve. If the lack of focus is your problem in life then there can be nothing better than mindfulness for you. It is a practice that requires immense focus even in things that we do without paying any attention to, like eating and walking. When you are walking or eating mindfully, the whole process transforms.

Mindfulness and Mindfulness Meditation

Some people misinterpret mindfulness as the same as mindfulness meditation. Mindfulness is a way of life. It is a choice of life that you adopt in which you choose not to remain reactionary.

You make a conscious decision of doing everything with full awareness. In this way of life, there is no place for reactionism. Your life becomes very calm and composed. You become immune to conflicts as you develop an inner mechanism to deal with physical, emotional, and psychological stressors.

Mindfulness meditation is the way to learn to become mindful. Through mindfulness meditation, you can learn the ways to gather your focus and raise your awareness levels.

This book will help you in understanding the ways through which you can become more mindful in life. It will show you the tools to mindfulness and would also help you in doing mindfulness meditation.

Chapter 2: Your Way Into Mindfulness Meditation

Meditation, in an ideal setup, helps in calming the mind faster and better. It is very relaxing and refreshing. It gives you a chance to get over your worries, stress, anxieties and other such things that might lead to a panic attack.

When you are in a meditative state such feelings are not able to frighten you anymore. Meditate state helps you in becoming more observant of the things that are causing such emotions. Your power of discernment improves and you are able to easily negate unnecessary fears. However, most people find it very difficult to get into the meditative state faster. When they try to meditate, they start having numerous thoughts and are unable to focus. Some people get scared when they close their eyes to meditate.

This chapter will explain the ideal settings that can help you in achieving the meditative state faster. It will explain in detail everything that can help you in getting into a meditative state faster. From an ideal place to sit for meditation to an ideal diet, this chapter will cover every single detail important for helping you in the meditation process.

Importance of Ideal Settings for Meditation

With a calm and composed mind, meditation is a very simple and easy thing to do. However, most of us don't have the luxury of having a calm mind. Our mind is usually filled with millions of thoughts at the same time. It is stressed about unknown things. It is fearful of a lot more things. All these things make it very difficult to build focus. We have too many thoughts in our mind and we find it very difficult to control the thoughts when the eyes are closed. We tend to overthink even more when trying not to think anymore. If the state of mind is negative, a downward spiral starts even faster in the mind.

It implies, most people find it difficult to focus the mind on nothingness. The mind keeps wandering and never lets us focus. Especially, if we are stressed, anxious, worried, or in a panic-driven state, the mind would keep driving us here and there.

The simple measures and adjustments in your routine mentioned in this chapter would help you in calming the mind and becoming more mindful.

These are standard practices that help in focusing better and faster. Everything given in this chapter is a general guideline for making your meditation session more immersive, satisfactory, and successful.

However, this doesn't mean that you would have to stick to them for your whole life. As you practice more, you'll find it easier to get into meditative state faster even in new settings. You may not need the amount of calm you needed in the beginning to build focus. You may be able to do mindfulness meditate even while walking, lying down, running or doing other activities.

Mindfulness meditation is a way to establish a strong connection with your own mind. There is no perfect way to do this. As you practice, you keep getting better at the task. The purpose of this chapter is to introduce standard practices that would help you in achieving the meditative state faster as you learn to master the art of mindful meditation.

The Essentials

Place

Meditation is the process of peeping deep inside your mind. Mindfulness meditation helps you in establishing a strong connection with the mind and becoming more aware. However, the process to achieve this state is tough and requires focus. To this end, a quiet and peaceful place is the best.

Some people like to meditate in their homes as that ensures freedom from unnecessary disturbances. Whereas, others like more serene places like parks, mountains, and riversides. Wherever you are able to focus better, that place is the best.

However, while choosing the place of meditation you should keep the following things in mind:

It Should be Soothing

The place of meditation should have a calming effect on you. There are some places where you are able to feel more relaxed and calm. Such a place would be the best for practicing meditation as you would be able to put some of your worries at rest. This makes bringing your mind to focus on important things easier. Whatever place you choose for daily meditation sessions should provide you the peace of mind. Most people find it very relaxing to meditate in parks and other such places with natural scenic beauty. However, if you are a beginner, it is generally good to begin meditation at your home if you are doing it alone. You can feel more safe, secure, and certain at your home and wouldn't have the fear of getting disturbed by other factors.

Quiet

You wouldn't want your place of meditation to be chaotic, at least not in the beginning. When you close your eyes, momentarily you are trying to detach yourself from the outside world. However, your mind would try to resist this with its full might. Any kind of noise in your surroundings would prove to be a catalyst for distraction. You must ensure that your place of meditation is free of such unnecessary distractions. Choosing public places like parks has 'disturbance' as the biggest demerit. You can't control the amount of disturbance in your surroundings whereas at your home you can have great control over it. Once you start meditation on a regular basis, such questions would become inconsequential as you would be able to meditate at almost any place in the world without preconditions. The beauty of mindfulness meditation lies in the fact that it doesn't lay preconditions. However, you will have to train your mind to achieve this state. Therefore, in the beginning, it is always best to find a quiet place to meditate.

Easily Accessible

Meditation is one of the most soul-satisfying activities that you can carry out in a day. It helps you in relaxing and releasing your stress. It also enables you to become more mindful of the things happening around you. However, it is an art that needs to be developed and you would need practice for it. To this end, it is important that your place of meditation is easily accessible to you. Choosing a place where you can meditate as often as possible, preferably twice a day at least, is always the best. The more often you practice, the easier and more convenient it would become for you. While choosing a place of meditation you must keep this factor in mind.

Positive Energy

Most people find it somewhat strange but it is a proven fact that you'd find it easier to reach a meditative state at your regular place of meditation. This happens due to several factors. First, a regular place of meditation provides you greater mental peace and security. You are able to easily put your guard down and focus inwards. Second, the more you meditate at a particular place, the higher is the concentration of positive energy at that place which helps in building faster focus. Therefore, you must choose a place where you can meditate again and again without obstruction and disturbance.

- You must keep your place of meditation clean and free from any kind of clutter. Try to have a separate room for meditation in your home. If that's not possible due to space constraints then you can also pick a corner in your bedroom for the same.
- You must keep the place of meditation clean. You can also burn incense sticks or light candles at the time of meditation as this also helps in building the focus faster.
- Inform anyone else sharing the room not to disturb while you meditate.

Time

It is very tough to fix duration for meditation. In the beginning, some people find it difficult even to sit for 10 minutes straight in the meditative state as the mind tries desperately to divert attention to a million other things. However, with practice, people find it easier to meditate for much longer without reeling under the pressure of time.

Therefore, it is important that you keep practicing regularly. You should try to meditate as often as possible.

Early Morning

Early morning is best for meditation as the mind is relatively free of thoughts. It is very easy to build focus at this time. Physical as well as mental pressure is considerably low during this time. Early morning meditation helps you in keeping your mind calmer and composed during the day. You will have better control over your emotions and you'll feel more positive.

Just Before Going to Bed

Meditation just before going to bed can give your day a perfect ending. It is a time when you have no pressure of the day. Your mind can be stressed from the events of the day; however, meditation can help in releasing that stress too. Meditation at this time helps a lot of easing mental and emotional pressure of the events that may have taken place during the day. You get time to consciously discern the events that may have taken place in the day. It brings down your anger, anxiety, fear, stress, and worries. This meditation will help you in sleeping better and hence you'll be able to start the next day better. When the events of the past day have been consciously discerned, your subconscious mind doesn't keep overthinking about them and hence you'll have better sleep. Meditation at this time is great for resolving sleep disorders.

You should try to meditate at least twice daily. You can start with shorter meditation sessions and then keep increasing the duration of the session as you start experiencing the physiological and psychological benefits.

Whenever You Feel Stressed, Anxious, Worried, or Angry

Mindfulness Meditation for getting relief in situations of stress, panic, and anxiety can be done anytime and anywhere. You don't need any kind of special preparation or setup. You'd simply need to focus inwards for a short while and you'd feel great relief.

Mindfulness Meditation is one of the best ways to calm the mind. It is a relaxing activity in which you get a better chance to look at the chain of events causing the agitation in a reasonable manner. You get a wider angle view of the scenario and hence it helps in taking away fear, anxiety, anger, stress, and worries.

Duration

Some people give a lot of importance to the duration of meditation sessions. There is no doubt that the longer the meditation sessions are, the better will be the impact on your physical and mental health. However, it is important to note that more than the quantity of time, the quality of the meditation session is important. This means that even if your meditation sessions are shorter but you were able to reach the meditative state, you will have great results. If you keep sitting for meditation for longer periods but you aren't able to focus properly or your mind keeps wandering, your meditation session may not fetch results in the same manner. Therefore, more than the length of sessions, the focus is important.

- Start with shorter sessions
- Begin with breathing exercises and don't fret much about controlling your thoughts. Eventually, you will get there.
- Don't try too hard to do things the right way, simply focus on meditation regularly. Perfection would automatically come with time.
- Practice meditation daily for at least 48 days. This is usually the time required for forming strong habits.
- Initially, you can use an alarm clock for keeping track of your meditation sessions. When eyes are closed, the time seems to pass very slowly and even in a couple of minutes you may start feeling that a lot of time has elapsed. This means you stand a risk of waking up from your meditation sessions very frequently. Having an alarm clock by your side helps you in staying in the meditation position for at least the required duration. As time passes, you'll overcome this hurdle and meditation would become a very easy and comforting activity, then the need for an alarm clock would cease to exist.
- Try to increase the duration of your meditation sessions slowly.

- You can do quick meditations of 10-15 minutes whenever you feel stressed, anxious, angry or worried. Meditation helps in easing the state of panic.

Clothing

When you are doing meditation, you want to completely focus inwards. It is a process that can get hindered by distractions. Tight or constrictive clothing can become such a distraction. Although there is no formal dress-code for meditation, loose-fitting comfortable clothes are the best for meditation. They help you in breathing easily and also don't cause distractions.

If doing meditation in your office wearing formal clothing, simply try to loosen it as much as possible. The purpose is to simply have complete focus inwards and not get distracted by unnecessary things.

The Posture

Several meditation techniques lay great emphasis on the correctness of posture. They are very particular about the way you sit in the meditative position and there are very strong reasons behind it. Meditation and Yoga are part of the same system. If your posture is correct, it gets easier to focus the mind inwards. Hence, your gains increase several times. Kundalini meditation, chakra meditation, Zen, and Yoga Meditation are some of the forms of meditation that give great importance to posture.

However, for new practitioners, sitting in complex positions can be tough. It may keep their mind focused on the position itself and they'd not be able to focus on their mind. Such people don't need to worry too much about the posture and should focus on being mindful and their meditation.

The inability to sit in a certain position shouldn't take away the amazing benefits of meditation from you. Even if you find sitting in certain positions difficult you shouldn't stop practicing meditation. Mindfulness meditation can be done while lying, sitting, standing, walking, or running. It is your awareness or mindfulness that's most important here.

Although you can choose any comfortable posture for meditation, there are some important things that you must keep in mind.

Important Tips

Keep Your Spine Straight

It is very important to keep the spine straight irrespective of the posture of meditation. Distraction, discomfort, and backache are some of the side-effects of slouching the back. You must always remain mindful of your back posture. If needed, you can even use a backrest as some people start feeling discomfort in sitting straight for long. However, slouching must be avoided at all costs.

When your back is straight, it is very easy to keep your mind focused. Slouching happens when you simply start floating in your thoughts. There are several disadvantages of not keeping the back straight.

- When you are bending forward a little while doing meditation, your mind will have all kinds of depressing thoughts. If you are doing meditation to get away from depression and anxiety, this could be a poor way to achieve that.
- If your body is tilted backward, you may have thoughts that will leave you restless. All the thoughts that you have been trying to avoid would come rushing into your mind.
- If your body is tilted to your right, it will lead to a feeling of lethargy. You will start feeling lazy pretty soon and would simply want to end the meditation.

- Leaning the body to the left is also equally bad as it increases sexual desires in your mind. You will not only have sexual desires but would also want to indulge in impulsive things.

It is always the best to sit upright with your back straight. You don't need to stress yourself, simply avoid slouching.

Keep Your Shoulders Straight

People usually misunderstand this point. Keeping the shoulders straight doesn't mean that you have to remain in the military attention positions with shoulders strained. It simply means that both your shoulders would be at equal height. Although this may sound childish, most of the time we tilt one of the shoulders unknowingly. This would give your body a sideway tilt that you'd want to avoid.

There is no need to keep the shoulders stressed. Simply remain aware of the position of your shoulders and keep them straight.

Never Use a Neckrest While Doing Meditation

You must keep your neck straight and must also avoid using any kind of neck rest. Keeping the neck straight helps in maintaining active control of the thoughts. If you are not keeping your neck straight intentionally, you'll be at the risk of drifting into sleep while doing meditation. It is an active measure to prevent dozing off.

Keep Your Chin Raised a Little

Keeping the chin raised a little bit also helps in getting into the meditative state faster. If you keep your chin tilted forward, there is a risk of feeling neck pain. You don't need to raise your chin too high. A minor upward tilt would do the job.

Keep Your Hands Rested Comfortably

You can either keep your hands comfortably rested in your lap or you can also keep them on your knees. Find the way you feel most comfortable.

You Can Use Comfortable Mat or Cushion

Comfortable seating is very important as you might sit for long periods in the meditative state. It is always best to choose a comfortable mat or cushion. Choose a comfortable chair if you want to meditate while sitting on a chair. If you wish to meditate in lying position, the mattress shouldn't be too soft as that can lead to bending of the spine.

Your Feet Must Remain Firmly Rested on Ground

In case you want to meditate while sitting on a chair, look for a chair that helps you in keeping your back straight. In case you are sitting on a chair, you should ensure that you're the soles of your feet are rested fully on the ground and your knees are straight. This helps you in remaining more mindful and also prevents slouching of the spine.

Don't Stress Your Body and Mind

Meditation is a very relaxing activity. You don't need to take stress or get tensed about anything while you are meditating. Simply keep your back, shoulders, and neck straight so that you remain completely mindful of the activity. Don't worry much either about time nor about posture. As long as you are able to remain mindful and focused, you are on the right track.

Common Meditation Postures

Chair Meditation- Meditation Sitting on a Chair

This is one of the most comfortable positions for people new to meditation. It is the easiest position and suitable for people across all age groups. You can do chair meditation sitting in your office, home, or even public parks with no hassle or preparation involved. This position is also great for people suffering from anxiety or panic attacks as they can quickly get seated and focus on their minds.

To begin chair meditation, you must keep the following things in mind:

- Sit in a comfortable chair with your back upright
- Adjust the height of the chair to ensure that your feet are firmly resting on the ground
- Your shoulders should be straight
- Raise your chin a little bit upwards
- Keep your neck straight
- Lay your hands in your lap or keep them on your knees
- If needed, you can also use a backrest to prevent slouching of your back

This is one of the best positions for beginners as it helps them in developing the habit of sitting in a meditative position without having to fret about complex postures. They get used to sitting for longer durations and transition to various other meditation poses becomes easier. You can do meditation in this position anywhere and at very short notice and hence it adds a touch of convenience too.

The Burmese Position

This is a very easy position. Anyone can do it easily

- Sit on a cushion in a cross-legged position
- Back of your feet should be facing towards the mat
- Place your hands in your lap
- Keep your back straight but relaxed
- Your neck should be straight
- Your head should be balanced
- Keep your shoulders straight but relaxed

Lotus Positions

Lotus positions are greatly preferred by meditation practitioners all over the world and there are very strong reasons for that. Often when you meditate, you might start feeling wobbly. People also feel that they don't have great stability and face difficulty in maintaining their focus for long. All these issues can be handled by sitting in lotus positions. These positions help you in forming a strong bond with your roots. You feel firmly grounded and hence trivial fears go away easily.

If you are trying to do meditation for tranquility, peace, and inner consciousness, these positions can help you a lot. However, it is a fact that people who have been doing yoga for some time or have been involved in sports would find it much easier to adapt to these positions. But, even if you find the lotus positions difficult in the beginning, there is no need to panic or feel sad. There are several lotus positions that are not very difficult and hence you can try them easily. You can start with easier postures and then experiment with the tougher ones to find the right fit.

To attain your prime objective in meditation, it is important to sit steadily and comfortably. While you meditate, you are trying to figure out the bigger questions of your mind, if your body keeps poking you like a small kid after every few minutes, you will not be able to meditate properly. Hence, it is important to find a posture that suits you the best. Initially, don't go for the tough one, choose the one in which you can sit easily. Over a period of time, you will be able to sit in the advanced positions automatically. You should simply learn to sit unperturbed by your body for any amount of time you wish to.

Quarter Lotus Position

Among the traditional meditation postures, this position is the easiest. You can sit in this position for long periods without feeling any significant discomfort and most people can sit in this position easily.

- Sit in a cross-legged position
- Place one foot in the crease of the other thigh
- Your other foot will rest on the mat under the knee
- Keep your back straight but relaxed
- Place your hands on your knees or in your lap
- Your neck should be straight
- Your head should be balanced
- Keep your shoulders straight but relaxed
- Try to feel if there is tension in any part of your body and ensure that it is relaxed

This is another easy position for beginners. You can use a cushion to make your seating arrangement more comfortable. This position helps in attaining the meditative state faster and connecting to the roots. Once you have become habitual of sitting in the meditative position, you must try this position.

Half Lotus Position

This position is also an extension of the earlier position. It isn't very difficult to implement and it helps you in remaining fully aware of your activities all the time. You should try this position once you have got accustomed to the quarter lotus position.

- Sit in a cross-legged position
- Place one of your foot on the top of the other thigh
- The other foot would remain under your legs resting on the mat or cushion
- Keep your back straight but relaxed
- Place your hands on your knees or in your lap
- Your neck should be straight
- Your head should be balanced
- Keep your shoulders straight but relaxed

This position helps you in achieving greater concentration and you also remain aware of your body while you meditate.

Full Lotus Position

This is one of the most powerful positions in meditation. This posture gives you great stability and helps you in remaining firmly grounded in reality. Your chances of drifting into sleep or unreal things go down considerably. Yogis and Buddhist monks have been practicing meditation in this position for thousands of years.

- Sit with your legs straight
- Now hold your right foot and place it firmly on your left thigh
- Hold your left foot and place it firmly on your right thigh
- Now place both your hands in your lap on top of each other
- Keep your back straight but relaxed
- Place your hands on your knees or in your lap
- Your neck should be straight

- Your head should be balanced
- Keep your shoulders straight but relaxed

This is called the basic posture. Experts say that the body finds it very easy to get into equilibrium in this posture. The respiration improves in this posture and hence the functioning of the heart and lungs also improves. This posture is also very good for calming the mind.

Seiza

This posture is very helpful for people who start feeling drowsy very fast. If distraction, laziness, and lack of focus is your problem, you should try this posture.

This position is very good for digestion and hence you can sit for meditation in this position at night. It will improve your digestion and you may get rid of several digestive issues.

- Sit on your knees with your legs stretching at the back
- The left big toe should be on top of the right big toe and the heels should be tilted apart
- The gap between your knees should be around two fists
- Rest your hips on your feet
- Place your hands in your lap
- Keep your back straight but relaxed
- Your neck should be straight
- Your head should be balanced
- Keep your shoulders straight but relaxed

The Standing Position

Mindfulness meditation can also be done while standing. The main focus of this meditation is to raise your level of consciousness and hence there are no barriers of position. As long as you are maintaining a healthy posture, you can do it in virtually any position.

While you do mindfulness meditation in standing position, you must keep the following things in mind:

- Keep your whole body straight
- You don't need to stand in attention but your body needs to have the balance
- Place your feet shoulder-width apart
- Your spine must always maintain its natural curve and should be erect
- Your shoulders should be firm
- Keep your neck straight
- You can fold your hands or keep them straight as per your convenience
- Your feet must be firmly grounded as many times you may feel shaky

This meditation position works if you want to immediately control your ebbing anger. If you are feeling very emotional or impulsive, then also this position is very effective. Standing meditation sessions are generally short and initiated to get over the rush of emotions.

Walking Meditation

The Buddhist Zen traditions believe that meditation needs to be a way of life. Therefore, Zen monks learn to meditate in every position. Walking is one of the most soothing activities. Mindful walking helps in processing the thoughts and getting over emotional curves. Mindfulness meditation while walking can open the doors of immense possibilities for you. It will help you in better processing of your thoughts and emotions. It will tremendously improve your decision-making process. It will also help in calming your mind and facilitate the growth of positive thoughts.

There aren't many rules for this meditation besides the usual ones.

- You must remain fully conscious of your body and mind.
- You must do mindful walking at safe places like in your room or gardens
- You shouldn't do mindfulness walking in crowded or congested places
- There is a difference in mindful walking and walking lost in thoughts. You must remain fully aware of your thought process and should have active control over it
- Your focus should be on resolving negative thoughts and emotions

Lying Down

You can practice mindfulness in any position and hence lying down is no exception. It is a position that's very relaxing for most of us unless someone is facing severe back problems and have problems lying down straight.

Although this position is simple and easy there are certain limitations involved. People stand at a very big chance of drifting off to sleep while they are trying to meditate. Your body is in an open position and hence the circulation of energy is not very efficient in this position. Yet, this position can be very helpful in focusing on the problems of mind at resolving emotional issues mindfully.

- You must lie down straight on a flat surface
- The mattress should provide adequate support to your spine and shouldn't allow bending of the spine
- Keep your hands straight beside your body
- Keep the palms of your hands facing down
- You can also place a thin pillow under your neck or feet
- At all times, you must remain fully aware or mindful or you'll drift into the semi-conscious state or sleep

Learning to Focus Inwards

Building inward focus is among the prime objectives of mindfulness meditation. It helps you in becoming fully aware of your body and mind. You are not searching here to look for the answers of the universe although some people are on that quest too. You are simply looking for the answers to the complications in your heart and mind. All these answers can be found if you are able to focus inwards completely.

This involves 3 important steps:

1. Steadiness of Body
2. Rhythmic Breathing
3. Relaxation

Steadiness of Body

While doing meditation it is very important to maintain the steadiness of the body. When you try to focus your mind inwards, you will even feel minor twitches in your body very prominently. This happens because your mind has less space to wander. It becomes more aware of the body. The twitches and sensations have always been there, only your focus was divided on so many things that they were never felt so prominently.

However, your focus should still not be your body but your mind. You must try to feel every sensation in your body and acknowledge it. Simply feel the sensations and let the urge to itch, rub or scratch go away. Your objective should be to maintain a steady posture. The less attention you pay to your physical urges, the greater the focus you will be able to have towards your mind.

Once you acknowledge all the sensations in your body and pass the urge to do anything about them, you will feel calm stillness prevailing. Peace in the body is very important for finding peace inside your mind. This is the reason, meditators all over the world give so much importance to posture.

In the old meditation traditions, this is called 'Asana Siddhi' or conquering the posture. Once you have complete control over your posture, conquering the mind will become easier as you will have one less thing to take care of.

Rhythmic Breathing

Breathing is one of the most essential acts of life. We seldom pay due importance to this crucial act. You can survive for much longer without many important things in life. However, surviving even for a few minutes without breathing is impossible.

The act of steady breathing can help in calming your body and mind completely. As much as breathing through the nose and keeping it steady can help in calming even the most agitated minds. When you become fully aware of your breathing, you realize that this simple act of inhaling and exhaling the air holds the key to life.

The second step towards building an inward focus is to do rhythmic breathing. Simply inhale and exhale while being fully aware of the breath you take. Don't rush the air you breathe. Let your breathing take its natural steady pace. It helps in relaxing you and calms your mind. The more you pay attention to it, the more rhythmic it will become. Smooth breathing will be deep and slow.

You simply need to keep your focus on this breathing pattern. Breathe in and breathe out. Maintain a natural pace. Don't try to force your breathing or to alter its pace. Let it become completely normal and dense.

When your mind is completely focused on breathing, your attention gets away from the racing thoughts in the mind. Your whole nervous system starts calming down. Even if you are having some stray thoughts in your mind, simply acknowledge them and bring back your attention to your breathing pattern.

Relaxation

When your body is still and you are breathing at a natural pace, you will find yourself in the best position to relax completely. The next step is to scan your whole body toe to head. Focus on each part of your body and try to find if there is any unusual sensation, stress, or tension in it. If you feel any part to be stressed or tensed, simply feel the tension dissolving in your mind and you will feel relief in that part.

Start from the top of your head to the tip of your toe and then backward. Acknowledge tension or stress in any part of your body and feel it going away. This will completely relax your body and you will have developed inward focus.

Building focus is a three-part activity.

In the first part, you make your posture steady. You acknowledge every sensation in your body and control the urge to take physical action. This gives you great control over your body and takes away your attention from external stimuli.

In the second part, you bring your breathing to a natural pace and this relaxes your body and mind. This simple act of bringing natural pace to your breathing will take away anxiety, stress, and worries. Your mind will get focused on the most essential activity for life. It will get a renewed understanding of the most important thing in life. It will understand that it still has complete control over one thing that is most essential for living.

In the third part, you acknowledge the stress and tension in any part of the body and help in easing it. This act will help in building inward focus completely as now external stimuli will not affect your awareness anymore.

Finding the Motivation

Seek Pleasantness of Mind

Meditation is healing. It helps in uncomplicating things or solving the complexities in your mind. Even medical science acknowledges the power of meditation these days.

Yet, modern life has become so hectic and complex that most people are not able to feel motivated enough to meditate. They keep suffering life in place of enjoying life. They remain caught up in the cobwebs of life but never take an initiative to free themselves that doesn't even require much effort.

Meditation is the easiest way to unlock the immense potential of your mind. If you feel that you remain unusually stressed or get agitated even by inconsequential things then meditation can help you in a big way.

If you feel that your mind is highly cluttered, meditation can help you in decluttering it. If you are getting emotionally hurt by the actions of people around you, meditation can provide stronger immunity.

Meditation is the way to solve most of your emotional and psychological riddles.

Above all, meditation is the way to bring ultimate pleasantness into your life. Most people feel that happiness can be bought with money to a great extent. They are wrong as even the wealthiest people in this world are caught up unhappiness in life. They also lack joy and pleasantness in life.

Pleasantness comes into your life when your mind is calm and composed. When it is not craving for things and feels completely satisfied, you'll feel ultimate pleasantness in life. This is a feat that can be achieved with the help of meditation.

Bringing pleasantness is life should be your motivation for meditation as this goal can solve most of the problems in life.

Mindfulness Meditation Techniques

Mindfulness is an act of cultivating awareness. You can become aware of any activity in life and you'll find great depths in it. Your perception of that very thing would change completely. For instance, we all eat food every day. It is a basic necessity of life. Yet, we seldom pay attention to the very act of eating. Most of us spend the better part of our eating in talking to each other, watching TV, or lost in the taste of food. Very few people pay attention to the whole process of eating. If you become mindful of the process of eating, you'll be able to see the whole process of eating differently. From picking up the morsel of food from the table to chewing it up, there are several important activities that take place. Most of them are important but we usually ignore them as we aren't paying attention to them. If you eat mindfully, you can prevent most dietary problems and your digestion would improve considerably. The simple act of chewing the food a certain number of times can matter a lot to your health.

Mindful meditation is the way to train your mind to become more mindful, aware and conscious. It helps you in learning the ways to live fully in the present in a non-judgmental way. Your brain gets rewired to make conscious decisions in every walk of life. From breathing to walking, your awareness levels in life improve considerably.

Body Scan Meditation

This meditation is an easy way to increase your consciousness level about your body. It can be performed lying down. This meditation helps in relieving not only the emotional and mental symptoms of stress but also takes away the physical symptoms of stress as well.

It requires you to lie down on a flat surface and mentally scan your whole body for any kind of stress in your body or mind.

You get a chance to mindfully sweep across or scan your whole body and acknowledge the things that have been causing stress. This simple mindful scanning of the body helps in releasing the built-up stress and makes you feel better. You get a chance to go through your feelings and emotions in a non-judgmental way and also see the way they are forming in your mind. The only thing that you need to remember while performing this meditation is to remain a mere observer and not try to change the train of thoughts or emotions. You don't have to be judgmental or form opinions about your thoughts. Simply look at their inception and development in your mind and try to unravel the cause.

You can perform this meditation easily any number of times in a day and it is very relaxing in nature.

Breathing Space meditation

This is a very quick meditation of a few minutes that can be performed anytime you feel agitated, scared, or anxious about anything. Our mind always tries to create a 'fight or flight' response in stressful situations to avoid them. However, the more you avoid fearful situations, the scarier they would become. This short meditation will help you in facing your fears bravely and get freedom from a restrictive life.

You can practice this meditation a few times every day. It requires you to become mindfully aware of the thoughts that are causing anxiety or stress in your mind. Most of the times we are continuously trying to push away unpleasant thoughts or ideas that may not have favorable results for us. This process also means that we also surrender the opportunity to get over them or conquer them. This meditation technique helps you in recreating that experience in your mind and looking at it deeply in a non-judgmental way. This process gives you courage and insight into the problem and you are able to overcome your phobias and frights. You don't remain scarred from certain things for the whole of your life. Facing your demons is the only way of defeating them.

You can perform this meditation by performing rhythmic breathing and looking at the experiences in a wakeful manner.

Movement Meditation

There are several Buddhist meditation techniques that are based on the principles of movement meditation. Buddhist meditation traditions believe that either we can do things mechanically as reflex actions or we can do them in a mindful way where we stress on the importance and consequences of every action. Even a simple action like walking is a part of this process as you'd be able to feel every step you take.

This meditation technique emphasizing on physical sensations as well as raised consciousness levels. You can even do this meditation while walking slowly. The only important thing is to become fully aware of every action you perform physically or mentally.

Expanding awareness Meditation

This meditation technique focuses on expanding the awareness level of every sense in the body. We have five physical senses and one spiritual sense. If you peer deep inside your mind and achieve certain stillness of body and mind, you can increase your sense of perception enormously. This meditation technique helps in using every sense to become more profound. The more deeply you stress on any particular sense, the stronger it becomes.

Usually, you can do this meditation in any position but the sitting posture is highly recommended.

Loving-Kindness Meditation

This meditation helps in fostering positive emotions and feelings. If you feel that you lack the feeling of gratitude, forgiveness, or acceptance then this meditation can help you a lot. This meditation technique helps in cultivating these feelings and you become more accepting and embracing. The feelings of love, care, and understanding find greater expression in you with the help of this meditation.

These feelings are always present inside us but many of us simply forget the art of acknowledging their presence. This meditation technique helps in igniting the lost spark inside us.

The main concept of mindfulness meditation is to acknowledge and accept the presence of various thoughts and feelings inside your mind but not to get involved in them. When you become a distant observer, even the most unpleasant thoughts can't cause any unpleasantness to you.

The Traffic Analogy

Understand this through a simple analogy of traffic.

If you are stuck in a huge traffic jam the feelings that immediately come into your mind are frustration, fury, anger, and anxiety. These feelings soon get taken over by desperation and helplessness. You start feeling miserable and even the most pleasant day gets marred by these feelings.

However, consider yourself lucky enough to have your residence on the top floor of a building from which you can oversee this traffic jam. Now imagine you have a cup of a steaming brew in your hand on a cold evening and you are simply looking at the hundreds of cars standing on the road. I can assure you that the thoughts wouldn't be that unpleasant anymore.

The traffic jam is the same. The only thing that changed is the way you perceive it. At first, you were feeling stuck, now you don't have any rush and hence you are able to enjoy the view.

When you practice mindfulness meditation techniques, you are able to train your mind to become unaffected from trivial inconveniences. It becomes equipped to handle stressful situations better and hence the level of pleasantness in your life increases.

Chapter 3: Learning to Become More Mindful

Becoming mindful is a process. You have to cultivate mindfulness in every aspect of your life. You must become mindful of your actions. As much as the simple process of breathing also requires you to be mindful. When you become mindful of your physical actions, your stress levels start to go down.

However, before anything else, you need to cultivate the habit of mindfulness mentally and emotionally. You can't do mindfulness meditation by simply sitting in the full lotus pose if your mind is not ready to fully acknowledge and accept the current state of affairs. Most of us keep reliving the life of the past. We carry heavy emotional and mental baggage from the past. We form strong prejudices that impair our decision-making skills. They make us judgmental and temperamental.

To become more mindful, you must follow the four approaches given below and your journey would become smoother and easier.

Cultivating Acceptability

One of the biggest hurdles of living in the present is not acknowledging and accepting the present. People like to live in the cocoons formed by them. Those are imaginary realms and hence they are living in them all by themselves. Their worlds don't match with others. This causes hurt and problems.

The first step towards mindfulness is to start accepting people, behaviors, things, and situations as they are and not like we want them to be. It is very important that we become more open and embracing. Even if embracing new things seems difficult to you in the beginning, you should at least start acknowledging their presence. Start acknowledging the things that you like and even the ones you don't. The same goes for people and behaviors.

Acknowledge your fears, phobias, and prejudices. Acknowledging them is the beginning of the move of accepting them. Slowly you would get the courage to face those fears as you wouldn't shy away from them.

The key here is not to look away when you face anything unpleasant. Let your mind analyze it objectively. Don't let your feelings of fear and despair cloud your judgment. The more mindfully you acknowledge such things, the easier it would get for you to face and conquer them.

Learning to Let Go

As a frank admission, this is a tough task. Most of us hang on to good and bad things in our lives. It is natural to hang on to good things but we find it difficult even to let the bad things go away. In a way, it is connected with our inability to accept or acknowledge them in the first place.

Now that you have acknowledged the things that may have kept scarring your mind. It is time to take baby steps to 'let go' of those things. This wouldn't happen all of a sudden. Simply accepting harsh realities doesn't make them any less fierce. The key here is to take baby steps towards understanding the cause of problems.

There are two types of problems in life. The first ones are those which we can deal with. The second ones are those over which we have no control. Most of the time when we are in an unmindful or cluttered state, we keep all the problems in the same box. This increases the number of problems we have to deal with.

- Mindfulness meditation gives you a chance to rewind your life like a video clip and try to understand the cause of the problems in your life.

- Don't begin with the toughest one.
- Don't pick the worst nightmare first.
- Start with the easiest problem.
- Learn the ways to acknowledge and handle those problems.
- As you get comfortable in picking and resolving the problems, you will encounter problems of both categories.
- Don't try to fight over every issue.
- Learn to identify issues over which you have no active control.
- Fighting or resisting those things will only create burdens and failures in life.
- Learn to let them go.
- Once you acknowledge the things over which you have no active control, It'd become easier for you to feel emotionally burdened by them.
- You get absolved of responsibility.
- This act can take away a lot of mental and emotional burdens.

The act of letting go can save you from inner turmoil. It prevents emotional outbursts and you become more confident, calm, and composed knowing fully well the things for which you can be held responsible.

Learning to Forgive

Of all the things that can cause hurt, the majority are the actions performed by others with complete disregard for your feelings or emotions. We get hurt and harbor the wound for as long as we can, not knowing that the wound is causing pain to us and not the culprit. This is another thing that causes the highest amount of anger, despair, regret, jealousy, blame and an array of such negative emotions.

The problem is that these things affect us the most and not others. We can keep the wounds fresh in our hearts and bear the pain or let the wound heal by forgiving them. The act of forgiveness is an act of kindness unto you and not on others.

Does this mean that you would keep forgiving everyone?

Would you present the opportunity to get wronged by everyone?

No, definitely this isn't the answer. Become more aware of the things that can cause such emotions. Try to avoid them as much as possible. Objectively analyze the things that lead to such emotions. If you have no control over them, let them go and forgive.

If you have control over the situation, make it well aware to others about your feelings. Keeping inside and fretting about is not going to take you anywhere.

You don't necessarily have to forgive others. You must forgive yourself for making mistakes, for causing hurt to others, for causing hurt to yourself and others.

Forgiveness is the best way to clear your mind of negative emotions. When you are forgiving in nature, you become soft on the mistakes of others and even on your own mistakes. You give yourself the rope you have been looking for.

Learning to Become Grateful

One of the biggest mistakes we are making these days is that we have stopped becoming grateful. We have stopped being thankful for the gifts we have. This single mistake is the cause of most of our miseries. We are so intensely focused on the things we want and we can't have that we stop respecting even the important ones we have.

In this world, more than 150,000 people die every day. A lot of unfortunate people will not be able to see the dawn of the next day. This means a lot more people lose their loved ones every day. It is a circle of life.

Yet, you are fortunate that you haven't been a part of those 150, 000 people. It is a big number, yet you weren't a part of it.

You are fortunate that even your loved ones haven't been a part of that number.

Someday, we will all become a part of that number, however, today is not that day. Isn't it a thing to rejoice?

Yet, every morning we wake up with no gratitude towards life.

- We wake up with regret that it isn't a weekend.
- We wake up with regret about getting late to the office or a meeting.
- We wake up feeling not so good.
- We wake with regret about the things we don't have.
- We regret the things we wanted but couldn't get.
- We regret not getting the dream education, job, house, car, spouse and a lot of other unfulfilled desires.

We are all living a life of regrets without paying any heed to the things that we have. We don't enjoy the beautiful things we have. We don't relish the power of taking a breath freely without the aid of equipment. Try to think of the value of that unhindered breath from a person fighting for a crucial breath.

This continuous life of regrets is the cause of most of our problems. We are crowded with imaginary problems. The things that are causing the greatest anxieties in our lives are not even important for the process of living. Yet, we start feeling as if life is worthless without them.

The moment we start cultivating gratefulness in our hearts, we free ourselves from this vicious cycle of negativity.

Learning to become grateful helps in finding pleasantness in every aspect of life. It is very easy to feel grateful by being mindful as you get an objective view of things.

You are able to clearly determine the priorities in life which generally get murky.

The feeling of gratefulness fills you with positive feelings and helps you in remaining happy and content.

If you are able to incorporate these 4 things in your life, becoming mindful will become very easy for you.

Chapter 4: Important Breathing Exercises

Breathing has a very important place in all kinds of meditations. Breathing helps in building quick focus and prevents diversion of mind. It is a very effective way to calm your mind and bring your focus to one point. This is a part of meditation that you will have to do from the very first day. Rhythmic breathing can play a very important role in quickly dissipating your anger, stress, and anxiety. When you breathe mindfully, you can actually help your body in lowering the blood pressure. It increases the flow of oxygen in the body and reduces the amount of carbon dioxide.

Relaxed Rhythmic Breathing

In this exercise, your complete focus should remain on your inhalations and exhalation.

- Your breathing should remain natural
- Don't try to force your breathing
- Simply become fully aware of every breath you take
- You must try to focus all your attention on the breath you take
- Feel its warmth
- Follow its path through your nostrils
- Initially, you may have distracting thoughts, you don't need to fear
- Simply acknowledge your thoughts and divert your attention back to your breathing
- Follow your inhalations and exhalations
- As you breathe with greater focus, your breathing would become deeper and slower
- Don't try to change anything or force your breathing pattern
- Simply try to find your natural breathing pace
- The more focused breathing you'll have, the calmer you'll get
- This is the best way to go into the meditative state

- Through this method, your mind becomes focused and you have better control over your thoughts and emotions

You can repeat this breathing exercise several times a day. Doing it early in the morning in fresh air is the best. This rhythmic breathing would help you in calming the mind chatter. You'll be more at peace in your mind. It is also a great exercise to relax and relieve stress. If you want to practice the steadiness of the body and mind, then also this breathing exercise is very helpful.

Pranayam or Breathing through Alternate Nostrils

This is one of the most popular breathing exercises advised in yoga. It has tremendous health benefits and it also helps in bringing focus and clarity of mind. This exercise is simple and can be performed in the morning and evening hours.

- Sit in the meditation posture, preferably cross-legged
- You'll need to hold your nostril from one hand, choose your active hand for the same
- Place your other hand in your lap in a resting position
- Keep your back and neck straight
- Now place your thumb on one of the nostrils and close it
- From the other nostril inhale deeply
- Release the nostril covered by your thumb
- Now using your middle finger close the other nostril and exhale fully
- From this nostril itself, inhale deeply
- Cover this nostril now and use the other nostril to exhale and inhale
- This process needs to be repeated several times

This breathing exercise is excellent for your health and also for beginning your meditation sessions.

Controlled Breathing

This breathing exercise is helpful for releasing all the stress and tension from your body. This breathing exercise is used extensively at the beginning of meditation to release the accumulated stress in the body and for bringing the mind to focus.

- Sit in the meditation position
- Inhale deeply
- Take in as much air as you can
- While you inhale, remain mindful of the movement of the air through your nostrils
- Imagine the air to be a ray of light
- Follow the path it takes in your body
- Feel it filling your lungs
- Observe the expansion of your chest as the air fills in it
- Keep inhaling till you feel your gut has got filled with the air
- Now hold your breath for a brief moment
- Simply count till 5
- 1….2….3…..4…..5
- Now exhale slowly through your mouth
- Try to empty out all the air inside your body
- Feel your gut getting empties
- Observe your chest getting deflated
- Repeat the process several times
- While exhaling feel as if this air is going to take away all the stress, tension, negativity, and diseases from your body
- This exhalation should make you feel lighter

This meditation helps in building pinpoint focus on the activity of breathing. All the mental distractions go away as your complete focus is on controlling the breath.

These are simple breathing exercises that can help you a lot in building deep focus and they also help in achieving the meditate state faster.

Chapter 5: Practicing the Art of Mindful Breathing

This mindful breathing exercise will help you in relaxing your body and mind completely. You'll be able to build unwavering focus and steer away random thoughts. This breathing exercise is excellent for people who are troubled by random thoughts as soon as they close their eyes.

The main objective of this breathing exercise is to learn mindfulness. You will remain fully aware of your breath at all times and would control it consciously. You will stabilize your breathing rate and control your breathing pattern too. This breathing exercise is also very helpful in easing tension and stress. If you are troubled by disturbing thoughts, this exercise would help you in calming your mind completely.

When you sit for meditation don't start the exercise immediately. Get seated on the cushion or chair and try to ground yourself properly. When the eyes are closed, the mind would try to incite you. You might have some important thoughts in your mind. Therefore, simply sit for a few minutes with your eyes closed gently, if any such thought comes to your mind write it down before you begin the actual breathing meditation.

Mindful Breathing Meditation

Get seated comfortably on the cushion

Carefully inspect your surrounding

Clutter around you can cause distraction

Clear it right away and resume your seating position

This is going to be a very relaxing and fulfilling experience

Feel the cushion on which you are sitting

Feel your limbs

If any part of your body is feeling stressed, simply move that part a little

Focus on your spine, it should be comfortably erect

Your neck should also be straight

Close your eyes gently

Raise your chin a little bit

Keep your shoulders balanced and relaxed

You can place your hands in your lap or on your knees

Ensure that they don't feel stiff

With your eyes closed, lean a bit forward

Now, lean a bit backward

Tilt your body a little to the right

Tilt your body to the left

Now, bring your body to the center and find the most comfortable seating position

Once again ensure that your spine and neck are straight

Try to feel your head positioned on your neck

You must remain fully aware of your body

With your eyes closed, scan your whole body for stress in any part

Acknowledge the stress or tension and feel it reducing

Excellent!

You are now ready for the breathing exercise

With your eyes closed softly, Inhale

Do not show haste

Don't try to force the air in

Let your breathing be natural

This is a very relaxing exercise

Simply inhale and exhale

You have to simply observe your inhalations and exhalations

Breathe normally

You may see a white light at the center of your forehead

That is your focus

You have to keep your focus at this point of white light and keep breathing

Now we'll inhale deeply and exhale slowly

Take a deep breath maintaining your focus on the white light at the center of your forehead

Hold your breath for a moment

Count till 3

1….2…..3

Now exhale slowly

Your exhalation should be longer than your inhalation

Very Good!

Again, take a deep breath through your nostrils

Become aware of the breath you are taking

Feel the sensation the air creates at your nostrils

Follow the path of the air

Fill your lungs with air

Hold your breath to the count of 5

1…..2…..3…...4…...5

Exhale

The exhalations are relaxing

They take away all the stress in the body

They are making you feel relaxed and warm

You are feeling good

Repeat this process 3 times more

Take a deep breath

Become fully aware of the point of your focus and the inhalation

The longer the inhalation the better

Inhale to the count of 3

1….2….3.

Hold your breath to the count of 5

1….2….3….4….5

Now, exhale slowly through your mouth to the count of 7

1….2…..3…..4….5…..6…..7

Again, take a deep breath

Remain conscious of your breathing and your focus

Inhale to the count of 3

1....2....3.

Hold your breath to the count of 5

1....2....3....4....5

Now, exhale slowly to the count of 7

1....2.....3.....4....5.....6.....7

Again, take a deep breath

Breathe deeply

Inhale to the count of 3

1....2....3.

Hold your breath to the count of 5

1....2....3....4....5

Now, exhale slowly to the count of 7

1....2.....3.....4....5.....6.....7

Excellent!

Your mind is completely relaxed now

There is no rush

There is no hurry

Stress has no place in this territory

It is your domain now

Some random thoughts may come to your mind

If you are having thoughts

Just acknowledge their presence

Do not be perturbed by them

They can't meddle with your unwavering focus

Again, focus on your inhalation

We'll take a deeper breath now

As you inhale follow the path of the air you breathe

Just feel the parts it fills

You'll inhale slowly to the count of 7

1....2....3.....4.....5.....6.....7

Observe the air filling your lungs

Feel your chest expanding as the air fills it completely

Feel the inflation of your stomach as it gets filled with air

Hold your breath for a moment

Allow it to mix with your blood

This air will take away all the stress and negativity from your body

Now, release the air very slowly through your mouth

We'll count till 10 as you exhale

1....2....3.....4....5.....6....7.....8.....9...10

Rejoice the relief you are experiencing

It is an unmatched feeling

The air takes away all the stress and anxiety from the body

It is making you feel rejuvenated

You are feeling good

You should start inhaling once again

The inhalation would be long and slow

Feel it illuminating the path it travels

Count till 7

1....2....3.....4....5.....6....7

Observe the complete path the air travels in your body

Follow it closely

Intensely direct it to the parts with the highest stress

This air will take away all the stress from your body

It will make you feel light and relaxed

Be gentle but be firm

You are capable of controlling your life completely

You can't be dictated by random thoughts

Now, hold your breath

Let the air reach every part of your body

It is the life energy

It is the ultimate need

Release the air through your mouth very slowly

We'll count to 10 as you exhale

1....2....3.....4....5.....6....7.....8.....9...10

This air will take away all your stress

It will rinse all the tension

It will get rid of the useless thoughts troubling you

You are steady and firm

You have the complete control

You are in command

Feel the relief you experience on exhalation

That's all your stress and tension going away with each breath

You are completely relaxed now

Let your breathing return to normal

Don't try to open your eyes or move

Maintain your position

Simply let the air come and go through your nostrils

Don't try to control your breathing anymore

You are completely relaxed now

Breathe in

Breathe out

Breathe in

Breathe out

Breathe in

Breathe out

Breathe in

Breathe out

Breathe in

Breathe out

Bring your consciousness back to reality

Don't open your eyes yet

Simply try to experience your surrounding with your eyes closed

Feel the sensation air is making on your skin

Feel the warmth or the cold of the surrounding

Move your limbs a bit

Now open your eyes slowly

Remain seated in the same position for a bit longer

Try to feel if there is some tingling sensation in your legs

Feel the peace and calm

Rejoice stresslessness

Feel free to get up at your will.

Chapter 6: Initiation

These short guided meditations will help you in building focus and awareness. They have been designed to ensure that you have a pleasant and flawless meditation experience.

It is important to remember that every individual may have a different experience while beginning meditation. People can experience a wide variety of sensations like itching, tingling, aches, heaviness, or firmness. There is no reason for you to worry as most of these symptoms are simple diversions created by the mind. You have to simply acknowledge these symptoms and try to drive your energy in healing the symptoms.

Generally, there are 3 main feelings observed by people:

1. Neutral
2. Pleasant
3. Unpleasant

You don't need to do anything about these feelings. Simply acknowledge the sensations and become aware of them. The more mindful you become, your experience will start moving towards a neutral point.

These are short approximately 10 minutes long guided meditation sessions. Simply follow the lead and experience the bliss of meditation.

Body Scan Meditation

The objective of the body scan meditation is to raise your awareness levels about the physical body. This meditation session will help you in vividly scanning your physical body through your senses. You will be guided to visualize various parts of your body to look for symptoms of pain and stress.

This meditation is helpful in not only relieving emotional and mental stress but it also brings down physical stress. You are able to connect to your body in a very powerful way.

Body scan meditation can be performed while sitting on a chair or lying down. Whichever position you choose, it must be comfortable for you as the purpose of this meditation is to provide complete relaxation.

Through this meditation:
- You will be able to explore ways to deal with physical pain
- You may find the link between emotional stress and physical pain
- You may also learn the ways to address emotional issues through physical relaxation

Preparation
- Either lie down or be seated in a comfortable position
- You can also choose to do it in a standing position
- You don't need to keep any part of your body stiff
- You should be in as much relaxed physical state as you can
- Close your eyes gently
- If you are sitting in a chair, keep your back comfortably erect but not stiff
- If you are lying down, you can use a neck rest to support your head

Meditation

With your eyes closed, try to observe your breathing pattern

Don't try to make changes to it or to control it

Simply observe the way you are breathing at the moment and try to find a pattern

Start taking long, slow, and deep breaths

Every inhalation should be through your nose

Every exhalation should take place through your mouth

The exhalations would be longer than inhalations

Try to observe the noises coming from the surrounding area

Even the slightest noise

The noise made by a fan

Even the noise made by a wall clock

If there is any noise acknowledge it

This noise will not be able to disturb you now

Take a slow and deep breath

Remain mindful of the whole breathing process

Feel the air passing through your nostrils

Experience it filling your lungs

Observe the air expanding your chest

The sensation of your stomach getting inflated due to the inhalation

Hold your breath for a few moments

Control your breath

This is the crucial moment

This is the time you will be in complete control of your mind

You might feel some warmth at your forehead

It is your awareness creating the sensation

Now, exhale very slowly

Don't rush through the process

Expel as much air as you can from your body

Empty out all the air from your stomach

Feel your stomach getting deflated

Feel the pressure at your navel

Observe the pressure at your chest

You'll feel more relaxed at this stage

You can repeat this process a few more times

Now, shift your awareness to your head

You may feel a tingling sensation at the crown of your head

You may not feel anything, that's alright

There is no need to worry

Simply scan the crown of your head through your inner eyes

Try to feel if there is any stress or tension in this area

If you feel any stress in any area throughout the exercise

Imagine it slowly dissipating

Bring your focus to your forehead now

To the spot between your eyebrows

Try to see the white light at this place

It is your focus at the moment

Feel if there is any stress at this point

Try to find if there are worries

If yes, feel then going away

You may experience random thoughts at this point

Thoughts are natural

You don't have to resist them

Simply look at the kind of thoughts originating at this time

Are they pleasant thoughts, unpleasant thoughts or neutral thoughts?

Simply look at them

Don't engage

Don't try to alter them

Don't participate

The thoughts are not the concern here

Acknowledge them and move forward

Shift your attention to your eyes

Scan the eyes for stress or tiredness

Throw some healing light of your focus on this area

It will help

Bring your focus down to your nose

Feel the breathing process

Observe the steady breathing

Do you feel anything abnormal here?

Shift your focus now to your ears

Feel if they are feeling warm

Is there any stress in your ears?

Scan them and move forward

Scan your mouth

See if your jaws are tightly clenched or open

Is there any strain?

Relax your jaws and move downwards

Shift your focus to your neck

Is there any pain or stress in your neck?

It is holding your head straight

Does it feel stiff or strained?

Bring your focus down to your shoulders

Feel if the shoulders are strained

Try to relax your shoulders a little more

Scan your collar bone

Is there any pain in your collar bones?

Is there any stress?

Send some soothing waves of your focus to this point

Bring your focus down to your chest

Feel the sensation of the pumping heart

Try to feel if there is any stiffness in this area

Try to observe if there is any pressure at the center of your chest

You can be having several thoughts at the back of your mind

Don't ignore them

Try to observe those thoughts too

Don't rubbish those thoughts completely

Simply look at them as a spectator

Don't get indulged with them

Now move your attention to your navel

Look for any stress in the navel region

Do you feel any pressure here?

If there is any pressure or pain in this area

Bring your healing focus to this point

Move ahead to your pelvic region

Try to feel if there is any kind of pressure in this area

Feel your pelvic region

Feel the places that are touching your bed or cushion

Become fully aware of this region

See if there is any pain, pressure, or stress in this region

Simply notice the sensation

You don't need to do anything at this point

Just remain aware

All sensations are temporary

Nothing is permanent

Even if there is some discomfort it will go away

Shift your focus to your thighs, knees, calves, and ankles

Try to feel any kind of stiffness in the muscles in your thighs

Observe the sensations in these areas closely

If there is any discomfort, simply acknowledge it

Try to feel it going away

Every breath that you are drawing own, feel the stress going away with it

It is a very relaxing feeling

Now, shift your focus to your feet

From your heel to the toes

Try to feel every part of the body

If there is any stress, make it go away with your healing touch

Now, you have observed your complete body

Try to look at it as a whole

Feel if there is any pressure, stress or pain in any part of your body as a whole

Rescan your whole body quickly

Move your consciousness from toe to tip once again

You'll feel very relaxed and rejuvenated

Now, become fully aware of your breathing pattern

Feel your inhalations and exhalations

Breathe in

Breathe out

Breathe in

Breathe out

Breathe in

Breathe out

Breathe in

Breathe out

Breathe in

Breathe out

Maintain your position for a few more minutes

Try to feel the external sensations once again

Do not open your eyes yet

Simply observe your surrounding through your other senses

Try to feel if there is any kind of unpleasant sensation in your body

Now you can gently open your eyes

Breathing Space Meditation

Breathing space meditation is best for relieving stress and anxiety encountered at any specific time. It is a short meditation that helps you in facing your fears and avoiding flight and fight response. This meditation empowers you to become stronger and bolder. You get the courage to face negative emotions and turbulent situations.

Stress and anxiety have an overpowering effect. Once a person is under the control of such emotions the responses are usually automated. This means that the victim loses the options to make conscious decisions. The victim simply repeats the past actions and never takes any real step towards facing the problems. Breathing space meditation helps you in acknowledging and understanding your fears and enables you to face them.

If you get stressed frequently and encounter issues in facing problems then this meditation can work wonders for you. It is simple and easy. It doesn't require much preparation and it is relatively short. It can be done anywhere.

Through this meditation:

- You will be able to face your fears
- You'll become stronger and bolder
- You'll get the courage to solve problems

Preparation

- Either lie down or be seated in a comfortable position
- You don't need to keep any part of your body stiff
- You can keep your eyes closed or if you are in a really anxious state you can also keep your eyes open
- In case you choose to do this mediation with your eyes open, choose a spot at least 5 feet apart to focus
- If you are sitting in a chair, keep your back comfortably erect but not stiff
- If you are lying down, you can use a neck rest to support your head
- It'd be much better if you can sit in a cross-legged posture as it will help in keeping you grounded firmly
- Connection with the ground helps in fighting fear, panic, and anxiety

This meditation is generally divided into 3 parts:

1. Acknowledging the fearful and negative emotions. Identifying those emotions and your reaction towards it.
2. Getting out of the autopilot mode and stop reacting mechanically. You will have to ground yourself in reality and become aware.
3. Expanding consciousness to a greater level so that you become more empowered.

Meditation

Sit in a cross-legged position or you can also sit on a chair

If you are sitting on a chair, keep your feet firmly rested on the ground

Place your hands in your lap

Close your eyes and turn your focus inwards

You can also choose to keep your eyes open and set your focus in front of you

You must begin with mindful breathing at first

Focus your attention to breathing

Don't try to make changes to it or to control it

Simply observe the way you are breathing at the moment and try to find a pattern

Breathe in

Breathe Out

Breathe in

Breathe Out

Take long, slow, and deep breaths

Every inhalation should be through your nose

Every exhalation should take place through your mouth

The exhalations would be longer than inhalations

Your complete focus should be on your breathing

Breathe in slowly

Feel the sensations the air passing through your nostrils is creating

Follow the breath

Feel its warmth

Observe the path it takes

Fill up the air till the brim

Hold the breath for a few moments

Let it mix with every cell in your body

Gently breathe out

Now, turn your focus inwards

Try to objectively identify the kind of emotions you are having at the moment

Don't be vague in your classification

Name the kind of emotions you are having

Are you feeling angry?

Are you feeling desperation?

Are you frustrated?

Is there disgust?

Are you feeling humiliated?

Whatever be the type of emotion that you are experiencing, you must categorize it

This single activity would help you in assessing the situation or emotion properly

Most of us are plagued with the ailment of poor judgment

We label even smaller problems as being larger than life and then keep buried under their burden

Correct identification would help in damage control

Simply, look at all the emotions floating in your mind

Objectively analyze the thoughts in your mind at that moment

You just have to look at them

The event has already happened

The damage is done

From here, things can only get better for you

Don't be afraid

Some daemons need to be faced at least once in a lifetime

You don't need to judge these thoughts and emotions

This wouldn't be the right time for that

You might have a clouded judgment

You simply need to identify them from a distance

Become aware of the emotions you are experiencing

Name each and every emotion you have at that moment

Anger, despair, frustration, hatred, humiliation, or any other emotion

You simply need to identify the emotion that's disturbing you

Now that you have identified the emotion specifically

Divert your attention towards any kind of physical sensation you are experiencing in your body

Scan the whole body looking for any particular area seeking your attention

You will have one emotion and a physical sensation in the body

You have identified that emotion with a physical sensation

We can now move to the second step

This step requires to focus on the breath

You must become aware of the present

The emotion identified by you is a result of an action of the past

You need to establish yourself in the present now

Become aware of your breathing

Don't try to alter your breathing

Simply observe it

Notice its rhythm

Try to feel the air being inhaled

What is the place where this air is creating the strongest sensation?

What is the strongest point where this air is felt in the body?

Do you feel it prominently at your nostrils?

Or you feel it when it fills your lungs

You must identify the area where the air is felt with the greatest intensity

Place your complete focus at that very point

If your mind feels shaky or keeps wandering

Simply pinpoint it and bring it back into reality

Don't be harsh

Don't resist a lot

Simply bring back your awareness every time your mind wanders

This will help you in keeping your awareness focused

You have now identified the emotions that have been causing the wreck

You have always found a way to keep your focus intact

Now, your final objective is to expand your awareness level

Your field of awareness should be beyond your physical self

Your whole body, aura, and expression should also become a part of it

Facing the problem as cosmic energy powered by your surroundings is a much easier task.

Feel the presence of this energy and get empowered

Stay in the moment for a while

Don't open your eyes immediately

Sit still for a while

Gently open your eyes when you are ready

Chapter 7: Relaxation

These guided meditations will help in bringing greater stability and peace of mind. These meditations have been designed for a longer practice. They will guide you in a step by step manner to achieve the meditative state faster. You can practice these meditations anytime to get relief from negative feelings like stress, worries, and anxieties.

Body Scan Meditation

Through this meditation:

- You will be able to explore ways to deal with physical pain
- You may find the link between emotional stress and physical pain
- You may also learn the ways to address emotional issues through physical relaxation

Preparation

- Either lie down or be seated in a comfortable position
- You can also choose to do it in a standing position
- You don't need to keep any part of your body stiff
- You should be in as much relaxed physical state as you can
- Close your eyes gently
- If you are sitting in a chair, keep your back comfortably erect but not stiff
- If you are lying down, you can use a neck rest to support your head

Meditation

Settle down in the position of your choice

Make yourself comfortable

Ensure that there is no physical discomfort due to your posture

When you are ready, close your eyes gently

We'll begin by looking into the mind

Just a gentle peek into the mind and the thoughts

You don't have to contribute

Simply observe the thoughts originating

Look at the random thoughts

Observe the way they are getting formed

Don't be judgmental about the thoughts

Simply have a look at the thoughts

Don't bother about their orientation

Don't fret about their nature

You don't need to dissect them at this point

There is no need for engagement

Simply look at the kind of thoughts emerging in your mind

Do you see any pattern?

There can be several random thoughts

You simply need to be mindful and thoughtful about the thoughts

See the way they arrive and the way they retreat

It is a learning experience

It helps in understanding that thoughts may not have the kind of significance we attach to them

Their origin can be very random

Now, focus your attention to your breathing

Don't try to make changes to it or to control it

Simply observe the way you are breathing at the moment and try to find a pattern

Breathe in

Breathe Out

Breathe in

Breathe Out

Take long, slow, and deep breaths

Every inhalation should be through your nose

Every exhalation should take place through your mouth

The exhalations would be longer than inhalations

Your complete focus should be on your breathing

Breathe in slowly

Feel the sensations the air passing through your nostrils is creating

Follow the breath

Feel its warmth

Observe the path it takes

Fill up the air till the brim

Hold the breath for a few moments

Let it mix with every cell in your body

Now gently breathe out

Repeat the process

Take a deep breath

Slowly and calmly

Follow it

Hold it for a moment

Now exhale even slower

You'll feel greater calm and relaxation

Every exhalation takes away the stress and tension in the body

Breathing in and breathing out is the key to bust the stress in any part of the body

Now return your breathing to normal

Don't control the pace of your breathing

Let it return to normal

Shift your attention to your feet

Through your mind perceive your feet

Try to feel the tip of your toes

Feel the gap between the toes

Try to observe any kind of sensation in your feet

Observe if there is any stress or tension in your feet

If you feel anything

Turn your focus to breathing

Breathe in the fresh air and breathe out the stress along with the air

Breathe in

Breathe out

Again, return your focus to your feet

Try to feel if there is still any kind of sensation there

Shift your attention upwards to the heels

Try to feel if there is any kind of sensation in the heels

Now, move your focus to your calves

Try to observe if there is any sensation in this part

If you can feel any stress in the muscles

Scan both your calves mindfully

Become fully aware of your body

Shift your focus to your knees

Ensure that there is no stress on your knees

Feel the knees through your focus

If there is any sensation return your focus to your breathing

Breathe in fresh air

Breathe out the stress in the body

Now, bring your focus to your thighs

Feel the thigh muscles

Try to observe any kind of sensation or discomfort in your thighs

Observe both the thighs carefully

Shift your focus to your pelvis

Try to sense any sensation in this area

If you are feeling any kind of sensation in this area

Shift your focus again on your breathing

If you feel any kind of desire or regret

Bring your focus to your breathing

Now, gently shift your focus to your navel region

The gut is the storehouse of many sensations

Try to feel if there is any discomfort or stress in this area

Observe the navel region carefully

Pay attention to the way the stomach moves when you breathe in and breathe out

Just observe the natural movement of your stomach

Try to feel anything unusual in this area

Move your focus upwards

All the vital organs are in this region

Scan overall health of this region

Try to feel the health and vitality

Shift your focus to your chest

Try to observe the heaving chest

Feel the rise and fall of the chest with every breath

Observe the beating of your heart

Try to feel if there is any stress or discomfort in this area

If you feel anything, shift your focus back to your breathing

Now, shift your focus to your shoulders

Try to observe if there is stiffness in the shoulders

Feel any stress or tension in the area

Move your focus to your arms

Feel both your arms

Try to observe any stiffness or discomfort in your arms

Pay attention to your arms

Feel the sensation of air on your arms

Remain mindful

Shift your focus to your hands

Feel your fingers

Try to feel the sensations at the tip of your fingers

Do you feel any tingling or other sensation?

If there is any feeling, shift your focus to breathing

Move your focus to your lower back

Try to feel any stiffness or discomfort in your lower back

Feel every part of your lower back through your focus

Observe any kind of sensation in the area

Focus on your spine

Feel the shape of your spine

Observe any kind of sensation in your spine

Move your focus to your upper back

Feel if there is any discomfort in the region

If there is any sensation, return your focus to breathing

Again, shift your focus upwards to the back of your neck

Try to observe the tension in this area

Feel the load the neck is bearing

Observe its connection to your head

Now, shift your focus to your throat

Try to feel any pressure or stiffness in the throat

Try to feel the passage of air through your throat

Remain fully aware of all the activities taking place in your throat

Move your focus now to the joint of your jawbones

Try to feel any stress in this area

Feel if this area is causing any discomfort

Shift your focus to your cheekbones

Observe your cheekbones

Now, try to observe your mouth

Feel if your lips are dry

Is there any stress in this area?

Move up to your nose

Observe the air passing through your nostrils

Follow the bone of your nose

Pay attention to the bridge of your nose

Now, shift your focus to your eyes

With your eyes closed, try to feel the eyes

Observe if there is stress in your eyes or around it

If there is any stress in the region, shift your focus towards breathing

Move up to your forehead

Try to observe any pressure in this region

Try to follow the white light in this area

Now, shift your focus to the top of your head

Try to feel any kind of pressure or discomfort in this area

You have completed the scan of your whole body

Now, look at your whole body one again

Scan the body from tip to toe

Try to feel any pain, stress or discomfort

Bring your focus to breathing once again

Maintain a natural breathing rhythm

Breath in

Breathe out

Breathe in

Breathe out

Breathe in

Breathe out

Breathe in

Breathe out

Breathe in

Breathe out

Maintain your position for a few more minutes

Try to feel the external sensations once again

Do not open your eyes yet

Simply observe your surrounding through your other senses

Try to feel if there is any kind of unpleasant sensation in your body

Now you can gently open your eyes

Mindfulness Meditation for Living in the Present

The objective of this meditation is to ground you in the present. It will gently help you in establishing yourself in the present. The first part of this meditation session will help you in relaxing completely. It will guide you through a breathing exercise and help you in becoming aware of your body. It will use body scanning as a tool to completely relax the body.

Once your body feels completely relaxed, it will provide guidance to get rid of all your stress and anxiety. It is baggage of the past being carried by the subconscious. This guided meditation session will help you in unloading the baggage.

Preparation

- Sit down in a comfortable position
- You don't need to keep any part of your body stiff
- You should be in as much relaxed physical state as you can
- Close your eyes gently
- If you are sitting in a chair, keep your back comfortably erect but not stiff
- If you are lying down, you can use a neck rest to support your head

Meditation

Gently close your eyes and focus your attention on your breath

Do not try to alter your breathing yet

Simply pay attention to the breathing pattern

Look at the rate of your breathing

Feel yourself inhale and then exhale

Breathing is such a simple process

It is the only vital physical process on which we have some control

Our heart keeps beating continuously but we can't control it

We have no control over our blood pressure

We have no power over the way our liver or the kidney function

But, we have the power to control our breathing

It is such a crucial process

We can't survive without it even for a few minutes

And, we have control over it

We can alter our rate of breathing

We will use this power of breathing to relax our body and our mind completely

Your rate of breathing is stable now

We'll now do deep breathing

It is one of the most relaxing activities

The more air we draw inside our body, the more energy it gets

It enables the body to draw out the stress

We'll take deep breaths

Hold the breath for a moment

Then we'll exhale slowly

Inhale deep and slow

There is no rush

Just let the air with all its life energies enter your nostrils

Feel it entering through your nose

Feel the sensation at the point of entry

Follow the path of air

Keep drawing it slowly

Fill up your abdomen with the air

Draw as much life energy into your body as possible

Now, hold your breath for a moment

Let the body infuse this air into every cell

Let the exchange of fresh air and used air take place

Breath out from your mouth slowly

The exhale would be even slower than inhale

Try to push out as much air from your body as possible

Let all the toxins, waste and spent energy go out of your body as possible

This will create space for fresh energy

Don't start inhaling immediately

Pause for a moment

The gap between the inhale and exhale helps you in realizing the beauty and power of this air

Inhale again

Long, deep, and slow

Feel the warmth of the air at your nostrils

Notice the sensation it creates when it fills up your lungs

Feel it fill up your chest

Fill your abdomen with the air

Hold the air for a few brief moments

Let it energize your body

Let it draw out all the negative energy from your body

The fresh air fills you with positivity

The spent air will take away all the negativity

Now breathe out slowly

The exhale needs to be slower

It needs to be longer

It will make you feel lighter

It will make you feel more connected and energized

It will help you in becoming grounded in reality

Let your breathing return to normal

There is no need to control your breathing now

Simply inhale and exhale

Slowly and gently

Shift your focus to your mind

Look at the thoughts emerging in your mind

Simply observe the thoughts

Don't participate

Look at the random thoughts emerging and going away

They aren't permanent

They aren't a reality

They are the creation of your mind

Your breathing is real

It is the only real thing

You are feeling relaxed now

There is no stress and anxiety

Scan your body from top to bottom

Start from your toes

Look for any stress or tension in your toes

Feel the sensation in your feet

Move upwards

Scan your calves

Feel if there is any stress in your calves

If there is any stress, acknowledge it and let it go away

Shift your focus upwards

Feel any stress or tension in your knees and thighs

If there is any, acknowledge it and let it melt away

Move your focus to the pelvis

Try to find any stress in the region

Try to feel any sensation in the region

If there is any stress, tension, or discomfort, don't ignore it

Acknowledge it and let it pass

It is a part of life

Become aware of all the sensations

Don't rely on memory

Feel everything at the moment

Shift your focus upwards

Scan your abdomen

Feel any sensation in the area

Acknowledge the stress and let it go

Move upwards to your chest region

Try to find any stress or anxiety in this region

Feel the way your chest is heaving

Shift your focus upwards

Scan your shoulders and the upper back

Try to find any signs of stress or tension in the region

If there is any, acknowledge it and let it pass

The more you acknowledge it, the less prominent it would become

Focus on your lower back

Try to feel stress in the region

Shift your focus to your arms

Feel if there is any stress in the arms

Acknowledge the stress in the arms

Let the muscles in your arm relax

Feel the comfort and relief in them

Shift your focus to your neck

Feel the pressure on your neck

Try to feel if there is tension in the region

If there is any acknowledge and release the tension

Shift your focus to the top of your head

Try to feel if there is any pressure in the area

Release any pressure or stress in the region

You are feeling completely calm and relaxed

There is no stress and anxiety

Your eyes are heavy

You are feeling very relaxed and composed

This is a beautiful moment

You are fully aware of your body and mind

You acknowledge all the problems and accept them

This is the moment of true relaxation

There is no running away from anything

Simply relax in the position you are

Feel the gravity

Feel fully grounded in reality

This is life

You are in complete control

Most of the times we keep fearing things that are inconsequential

We keep carrying things that are unnecessary

We all have the baggage of the past

We don't accept that it is past and we bring it into our present

The past keeps interfering in the present

It never lets you live in the present fully

You also have a backpack on

There is no need to carry the backpack

You are feeling that it isn't heavy

But, it is unnecessary weight

Let's go for a walk in the woods

It's a small trek

The woods are lush green

It rained yesterday

The ground beneath is soft

You have great sneakers

There is no problem with walking

Let's explore the woods a bit more

It is beautiful and dense

There are so many new trees and flowers

The greenery is mesmerizing

It is taking the breath away

There are flowers you haven't ever seen

The birds are chirping

You like the songs of the birds

There is a peculiar sound coming

You want to track it

You want to see the birds singing it

The direction from where it is coming has dense vegetation

But, you are feeling relaxed and pleasant

It is a good day to walk

There is no harm in exploring

As you move into the denser vegetation

Movement is getting difficult

The backpack is making it difficult to move

The branches of the trees are getting stuck in the bag

It is restricting your movement

You really don't need this bag

It is simply baggage of the past

Get rid of it so that exploring new things becomes easier

It will always keep you tied to the things that don't matter now

It will never allow smooth passage into the present

Let bygones be bygones

You have made up your mind

You'll let the bag go

You drop your bag

You can revisit it whenever you want

It is past

It will always be there

It can't be stolen or robbed

It has already happened

It is very easy to move without the bag

You are feeling light and free

Your pace has increased

There is no burden on you

You are floating like a feather

Ah finally, you have located the bird

It is as beautiful as its voice

Listen to it for as long as you want

It has started to drizzle

You like the rains

But, it is getting dark too

You should get back

Walking back is easy

There is no bag on your back

You are light

Let us get back to the awareness

Feel your body

Feel your breathing

Feel the sensations

It is good to be free of the baggage of past

You have your roots in the present

You are fully aware of your being

Let us get back to the breathing

Keep breathing normally

Breathe in

Breathe out

Breathe in

Breathe out

Breathe in

Breathe out

Feel your surrounding with your eyes closed

Relish the feeling of relaxation

Savor the moment of calm

Enjoy getting rid of the burden

You can open your eyes whenever you want

Mindfulness Meditation for Reducing Anxiety and Stress

This mindfulness meditation helps in reducing stress and anxiety. It will relax you completely and you will be able to get over your anxieties easily. You can practice this guided meditate whenever you feel anxious or stressed.

Preparation

- Either lie down or be seated in a comfortable position
- You don't need to keep any part of your body stiff
- You should be in as much relaxed physical state as you can
- Close your eyes gently
- If you are sitting in a chair, keep your back comfortably erect but not stiff
- If you are lying down, you can use a neck rest to support your head

Meditation

Sit in a relaxed manner

Don't worry about anything

Don't think much

Simply relax

The feeling of stress and anxiety are temporary

If you are feeling really anxious rub your palms

Rub them vigorously

Now put them on your cheeks

Feel the warmth of your palms

It is a very relaxing feeling

Now make yourself comfortable on the chair or cushion

Move around a bit on your seat

Adjust yourself completely

Feel if any part of your body is feeling a twitch or stress

You can move your arms or the body part to relax

When you get finally settled, we can begin

Sit with your back upright

Keep your neck straight

Hold your shoulders in balance

Position your chin bending a bit upwards

Now, Close your eyes

Become aware of your body

Become aware of your breathing

Try to feel if any part of the body is having an unusual sensation

Acknowledge it

Bring your focus to your breathing

It is one of the most important activities

However, you don't have to alter or control your breathing yet

Simply observe your breathing

Look at the beautiful process of inhalation and exhalation

Air going in and air coming out

Observe the frequency of your breathing

See if your rate of breathing is high

Let your breathing become completely normal

Simply,

Breathe in

Breathe out

Breathe in

Breathe out

Breathe in

Breathe out

You must have an unwavering focus on your breath

Don't try to think anything

Thoughts may still come

Don't pay attention to them

Only pay undivided attention to your breathing

If your mind gets diverted by random thoughts

Don't worry

Bring back your attention to the breathing

Now, we'll take a deep breath

Long, slow, and deep breath

Fill in as much air in your lungs as you can

But do it very slowly

Don't rush the process

Inhale slowly

Feel the life energy passing into your body through your nostrils

Imagine the sensation of the breath

The warmth it creates

Fill your body with this air to the brim

From your lungs to your gut

Fill everything with the air

We'll hold this air briefly

Then, we'll exhale even slower

Exhale through your mouth wide open

Make a deep sound while you exhale

Breathe in slowly through the nostrils

Fill the air till your gut

Relish the air for a few moments

Maintain your complete focus on the breathing

Exhale with a deep sound through your mouth

We'll repeat the process a few more times

Breathe in slowly through the nostrils

Fill the air till your gut

Relish the air for a few moments

Maintain your complete focus on the breathing

Exhale with a deep sound through your mouth

Again

Breathe in slowly through the nostrils

Fill the air till your gut

Relish the air for a few moments

Maintain your complete focus on the breathing

Exhale with a deep sound through your mouth

Again

Breathe in slowly through the nostrils

Fill the air till your gut

Relish the air for a few moments

Maintain your complete focus on the breathing

Exhale with a deep sound through your mouth

Once again

Breathe in slowly through the nostrils

Fill the air till your gut

Relish the air for a few moments

Maintain your complete focus on the breathing

Exhale with a deep sound through your mouth

Once more

Breathe in slowly through the nostrils

Fill the air till your gut

Relish the air for a few moments

Maintain your complete focus on the breathing

Exhale with a deep sound through your mouth

This breathing exercise helps in relaxing the body and the mind completely

It rejuvenates the body

Relaxes it completely

You are feeling very relaxed now

There is no stress or anxiety now

You don't have the time for that

You are feeling pleasant

Maintain your focus on your forehead

Look for the light

There is a white light

Look above your eyebrows

At the center of your forehead

It is a very soothing light

Pleasant and relaxing

Let's explore it closely

There is white fog around here

Enter into it

Let's see what's in it

You are feeling very light

It feels as if you are floating

You can't see the ground

There is so much fog underneath

But the ground is soft

It's cushiony

Feels like green grass

Soft and natural

It's very beautiful here

There is a white mountain far-far ahead

You can imagine its snow-clad peaks

There is a big ground

There is a valley underneath

You can see a river flowing in it

It's a clear river

The fog has cleared now

You can see everything very clearly

It's more beautiful than you had imagined

It's not a deserted place

There are kids playing at one side

You can also see some beautiful white sheep grazing

The kids are carefree

They haven't even noticed you

They are busy in their games

There is a steep cliff

You want to see what's under it

It can be risky

But you can be cautious

Move ahead

Explore!

The river looks so beautiful from here

You can see the silver streaks of the crystal clear water

The kids have also moved closer to you

They are still busy with their games

You are simply in love with the sight

You are feeling very light and relaxed

Wait there is some burden on your back

There's a backpack

Why are you carrying a backpack?

There is no need for it

Let's see the contents

What is making the bag so heavy

There are stones

Black and grey

Different shades of grey

Different shapes and sizes

All the worries and anxieties that you have kept stored in your heart

Some are petty ones others are big

Some are anxieties of your own making

Other are insecurities that you had

There are stones of anger, discontent, distrust, deceit

There are some stones of hurt, disbelief

But, who carries stones?

They aren't precious stones

They don't mean anything

Their weight would keep increasing

Their edges would keep getting sharp

They are a burden and a danger

It's better to unload it

You pick up a stone and throw it towards the river

It fell short of a few inches

You can do better than that

Pick up another stone

Weigh it properly in your hands

Judge the gap and hurl it

Bingo!

It fell in the river with a big splash

You've caught the attention of the kids now

They are looking at you

It's a game

There are no stones on this cliff other than these

The kids expect you to share

You offer them

They want to compete in this game

You pick one stone and the leader of the gang also picks one

And go!

Your stone went ahead

You are big and strong

Be proud of it

The other kids are also eyeing the stones

You have given them an open invitation

Everyone picks up a stone from the bag

Several kids throw the stones at ones

It's difficult to judge whose stone went ahead

But, the bag is getting lighter

There are only enough stone for one last round of stone-throwing

Everyone picks the stones

Yours went much ahead

This time you were much more confident

You didn't want to hold on to it

Good riddance!

The kids have started playing another game

It's just beautiful to watch them play

The sheep have also come near them

It's almost evening

Time for them to go

It's time to get back

Without the bag, you're floating like a feather

It seems as if there is weightlessness here

The bag was really heavy

You have been carrying it for a long time

Anyway, it's gone now

Let's get back

Get into the fog

It's the doorway to reality

Bring your focus back to your breathing

Let it stabilize

Simply,

Breathe in

Breathe out

Breathe in

Breathe out

Breathe in

Breathe out

Try to feel your limbs

Feel the external sensations on your body

The feel of the clothes against your body

Listen to the noises around you

Don't open your eyes yet

Simply relish the feeling of relaxation

The weightlessness

The end of anxiety

It is an amazing feeling

You can open your eyes now

Don't get up right away

Try to move your limbs a bit

Feel if there is any tingling sensation in them

You're free to get up now

Loving-Kindness Meditation

Preparation

- Either lie down or be seated in a comfortable position
- You don't need to keep any part of your body stiff
- You should be in as much relaxed physical state as you can
- Close your eyes gently
- If you are sitting in a chair, keep your back comfortably erect but not stiff
- If you are lying down, you can use a neck rest to support your head

Meditation

Sit in a relaxed manner

Don't worry about anything

Don't think much

Simply relax

Now make yourself comfortable on the chair or cushion

Move around a bit on your seat

Adjust yourself comfortably

You can move your arms or the body part to relax

When you get finally settled, we can begin

Sit with your back upright

Keep your neck straight

Hold your shoulders in balance

Position your chin bending a bit upwards

Now, Close your eyes

Become aware of your body

Become aware of your breathing

Try to feel if any part of the body is having an unusual sensation

Acknowledge it

Observe the frequency of your breathing

See if your rate of breathing is high

Let your breathing become completely normal

Simply,

Breathe in

Breathe out

Breathe in

Breathe out

Breathe in

Breathe out

Breathe in slowly through the nostrils

Fill the air till your gut

Relish the air for a few moments

Maintain your complete focus on the breathing

Exhale with a deep sound through your mouth

We'll repeat the process a few more times

Breathe in slowly through the nostrils

Fill the air till your gut

Relish the air for a few moments

Maintain your complete focus on the breathing

Exhale with a deep sound through your mouth

Again

Breathe in slowly through the nostrils

Fill the air till your gut

Relish the air for a few moments

Maintain your complete focus on the breathing

Exhale with a deep sound through your mouth

Think of a person who has always loved you

A person who always ignored your flaws

Who was never judgmental

Who showered unconditional love on you

The person who made you smile freely

In whose company you felt loved and cared for

That person can be alive or may have passed away

The memory of such loved ones is always alive

He/she can be anyone

Relative, friend, teacher, spouse

Imagine that person standing in front of you sending love and well wishes

Imagine that person wishing for your safety and happiness

Feel the sense of love and care you have received

Now say,

May I be happy

May I be at peace

May I be well, strong and healthy

May I be filled with loving-kindness

May I feel connected and Calm

May I feel the joy of being alive

Repeat once again

May I be happy

May I be at peace

May I be well, strong and healthy

May I be filled with loving-kindness

May I feel connected and Calm

May I feel the joy of being alive

Imagine yourself surrounded by all your loved ones

All of them are showering their love and affection on you

You are receiving the love and kindness of all your loved ones

They are wishing you happiness, health, and well-being

Repeat yet again

May I be happy

May I be at peace

May I be well, strong and healthy

May I be filled with loving-kindness

May I feel connected and Calm

May I feel the joy of being alive

Now picture someone you love dearly. Picture him or her standing in front of you. It's your turn now to send your love and well wishes to that person.

Wish with all your heart

Show your gratitude

Show some love

Show your affection

Repeat the following 3 times

May you be happy

May you be at peace

May you be well, strong and healthy

May you be filled with loving-kindness

May you feel connected and Calm

May you feel the joy of being alive

May you live with ease

Again,

May you be happy

May you be at peace

May you be well, strong and healthy

May you be filled with loving-kindness

May you feel connected and Calm

May you feel the joy of being alive

May you live with ease

Once again,

May you be happy

May you be at peace

May you be well, strong and healthy

May you be filled with loving-kindness

May you feel connected and Calm

May you feel the joy of being alive

May you live with ease

Now think of a few people whom you may not know very well

All those people who might have served you at some point or you might have interacted with them but never quite built an acquaintance

Servers in the cafes, clerks at the bank, watchmen, street-food vendor, a neighbor, a colleague or anyone else with whom you don't feel a strong bond but have no animosity

Everyone needs love and kindness

Everyone needs their share of affection and appreciation

Spreading love and gratitude will fill you with gratitude

You don't need to express this love or gratitude to them in person

Simply feel the love and gratitude from the inner corners of your heart

Say,

May you be happy

May you be at peace

May you be well, strong and healthy

May you be filled with loving-kindness

May you feel connected and Calm

May you feel the joy of being alive

May you live with ease

Repeat,

May you be happy

May you be at peace

May you be well, strong and healthy

May you be filled with loving-kindness

May you feel connected and Calm

May you feel the joy of being alive

May you live with ease

Once again,

May you be happy

May you be at peace

May you be well, strong and healthy

May you be filled with loving-kindness

May you feel connected and Calm

May you feel the joy of being alive

May you live with ease

Now think of the people who might not be on good terms with you

The people towards which you harbor negative feelings

Feelings of hatred,

Contempt,

Jealousy,

Apathy,

Disregard

These can be people who make you feel uncomfortable

They might have caused hurt to you

They might have deceived you

But, treating them as enemies is not going to do any good to you

They did something bad

They might be enjoying their lives

But, you are harboring negative feelings in your heart due to them

It is always better to throw away all the negativity

Let go of your anger and anguish

Even those people may need their share of love and well wishes

Let go of negative feelings and become forgiving

Mindfully pardon their mistakes and feel love and kindness for them

Say,

May you be happy

May you be at peace

May you be well, strong and healthy

May you be filled with loving-kindness

May you feel connected and Calm

May you feel the joy of being alive

May you live with ease

Repeat,

May you be happy

May you be at peace

May you be well, strong and healthy

May you be filled with loving-kindness

May you feel connected and Calm

May you feel the joy of being alive

May you live with ease

Once more,

May you be happy

May you be at peace

May you be well, strong and healthy

May you be filled with loving-kindness

May you feel connected and Calm

May you feel the joy of being alive

May you live with ease

You have now wished love and kindness for friends and foe

Let us now widen this circle

Increase the area of loving-kindness approach

Wish the same for all the living beings in your city, country, and the world

Wish everyone to be happy, healthy, and safe

Wish for everyone to achieve the goals in life

Wish prosperity for everyone

It isn't important to know a person to wish well for them

You need to know people to feel hatred and contempt

You can show love and kindness to the whole world without ever knowing or interacting with them

Say,

May you be happy

May you be at peace

May you be well, strong and healthy

May you be filled with loving-kindness

May you feel connected and Calm

May you feel the joy of being alive

May you live with ease

Repeat,

May you be happy

May you be at peace

May you be well, strong and healthy

May you be filled with loving-kindness

May you feel connected and Calm

May you feel the joy of being alive

May you live with ease

Once again,

May you be happy

May you be at peace

May you be well, strong and healthy

May you be filled with loving-kindness

May you feel connected and Calm

May you feel the joy of being alive

May you live with ease

Shift your focus to your breathing once again

Observe the frequency of your breathing

See if your rate of breathing is high

Let your breathing become completely normal

Simply,

Breathe in

Breathe out

Breathe in

Breathe out

Breathe in

Breathe out

Try to feel your limbs

Feel the external sensations on your body

The feel of the clothes against your body

Listen to the noises around you

Don't open your eyes yet

Simply relish the feeling of relaxation

The weightlessness

The end of anxiety

It is an amazing feeling

You can open your eyes now

Don't get up right away

Try to move your limbs a bit

Feel if there is any tingling sensation in them

You're free to get up now

Chapter 8: Practice Short 3 Minute Guided Meditation for Bringing Peace to Mind

Meditation

Sit in a relaxed manner

Don't worry about anything

Don't think much

Simply relax

Make yourself comfortable on the chair or cushion

Move around a bit on your seat

Adjust yourself completely

Feel if any part of your body is feeling a twitch or stress

You can move your arms or the body part to relax

When you get finally settled, we can begin

Sit with your back upright

Keep your neck straight

Hold your shoulders in balance

Position your chin bending a bit upwards

Now, Close your eyes

Become aware of your body

Become aware of your breathing

Try to feel if any part of the body is having an unusual sensation

Acknowledge it

Bring your focus to your breathing

It is one of the most important activities

However, you don't have to alter or control your breathing yet

Simply observe your breathing

Look at the beautiful process of inhalation and exhalation

Air going in and air coming out

Observe the frequency of your breathing

See if your rate of breathing is high

Let your breathing become completely normal

Simply,

Breathe in

Breathe out

Breathe in

Breathe out

Breathe in

Breathe out

Now we'll start slow inhalations

Hold the breath for a few moments

And very slow exhalation

If you get troubled or distracted by random thoughts, pay no attention to them

Don't be perturbed, distracting thoughts are common

There is no reason to worry about them

Observe the thoughts

Remain non-judgmental

Every time your focus gets diverted, bring it back to your breathing

If your mind is getting distracted repeatedly,

Continue breathing while counting in reverse

Inhale

Count down from 4

4...3...2...1

Keep your breath steady for the same duration

4...3...2...1

Now, very slowly release your breath through your mouth counting down from 7

7...6...5...4...3...2...1

Again

Inhale

Count down from 4

4...3...2...1

Keep your breath steady for the same duration

4...3...2...1

Now, very slowly release your breath through your mouth counting down from 7

7...6...5...4...3...2...1

Once again

Inhale

Count down from 4

4...3...2...1

Keep your breath steady for the same duration

4...3...2...1

Now, very slowly release your breath through your mouth counting down from 7

7...6...5...4...3...2...1

Relax

Breathe easy

Pan your focus on your breathing

Breathe normally

Become aware of your surrounding

You can open your eyes at will now.

5 Minute Guided Meditation for Building Focus

Meditation

Sit in a relaxed manner

Don't worry about anything

Don't think much

Simply relax

Make yourself comfortable on the chair or cushion

Move around a bit on your seat

Adjust yourself completely

Feel if any part of your body is feeling a twitch or stress

You can move your arms or the body part to relax

When you get finally settled, we can begin

Sit with your back upright

Keep your neck straight

Hold your shoulders in balance

Position your chin bending a bit upwards

Now, Close your eyes

Become aware of your body

Become aware of your breathing

Try to feel if any part of the body is having an unusual sensation

Acknowledge it

First of all, try to feel the cushion or chair on which you are seated

Try to imagine establishing contact with the earth

Try to feel if you are fully grounded or unstable

Now bring your focus back to your head

Look at the point above your eyebrows on your forehead

You may see some light there

The color of the light can be different for all

Simply try to look beyond that light

Do you observe any pattern, distinction, or heat?

Try to scan if there is any strange sensation in the body

Bring your focus to your chest

Try to observe the way your chest is rising and falling with every breath

The expanse of the chest is not the same

It isn't a controlled breathing

The body is breathing at its natural rhythm

You may notice that your thoughts are wandering a lot

It isn't a problem

It is the natural way of the mind to function

The mind can have thousands of thoughts at the same time

All thoughts may not require your participation

But, when you are trying to focus on something else, the mind will try to disturb you

It seeks your undivided attention

Your focus will shift from watching the breathing to various random thoughts

You don't need to worry about that

Simply observe the thought

Don't participate

Don't contribute

Don't criticize

Don't judge

Don't fret

Don't get frustrated

Simply look at it

And bring back your focus to your breathing

Initially, your focus may break frequently

Your mind is untrained

Your focus is weak

You will have to work on both

But, both are workable

We'll begin the breathing exercise now

Simply inhale and keep adding 1 till the count of 10

Once you reach the count of 10, count backward

If you ever forget the count

Resume counting from 1

If you have to repeat the process several times, don't worry

Simply keep repeating the process honestly

It is not about achieving perfection of breathing

It is an attempt to build a greater focus in life

It is all about avoiding distractions in life

Working while still there are several distractions

Inhale count 1

Exhale

Inhale add 1

Exhale

Inhale add 1

Exhale

Inhale add 1

Exhale

Inhale add 1

Exhale

Inhale add 1

Exhale

Inhale add 1

Exhale

Inhale add 1

Exhale

Inhale add 1

Exhale

Inhale add 1

Exhale

If you have to repeat this process several times over, don't worry

It is the part of the brain's training process

7 Minute Guided Meditation for Breath Control and Relaxation

Meditation

Sit in a relaxed manner

Don't worry about anything

Don't think much

Simply relax

Make yourself comfortable on the chair or cushion

Move around a bit on your seat

Adjust yourself completely

Feel if any part of your body is feeling a twitch or stress

You can move your arms or the body part to relax

When you get finally settled, we can begin

Sit with your back upright

Keep your neck straight

Hold your shoulders in balance

Position your chin bending a bit upwards

Now, Close your eyes

Become aware of your body

Become aware of your breathing

Begin with normal breathing

Simply become aware of your breathing

With your eyes closed, observe each breath closely

Follow the path it takes in your body

Feel the sensation of cold or warmth it creates at the point of entry

You must remain fully aware of your breathing

We will now begin deep breathing

You will inhale deep and slow

Hold it for a few moments

And then

Exhale even slower

Begin with

Inhalations to the count of 3

1....2....3.

Hold your breath to the count of 5

1....2....3....4....5

Exhale slowly through your mouth to the count of 7

1....2.....3.....4....5.....6.....7

Again, take a deep breath

Remain conscious of breathing and your focus

Inhale to the count of 3

1....2....3.

Hold your breath to the count of 5

1....2....3....4....5

Now, exhale slowly to the count of 7

1....2.....3.....4....5.....6.....7

This breathing exercise can help in relaxing your mind completely

Your focus becomes stronger and you are able to control the frequent swaying of thought

Resume breathing normally

Simply

Breathe in

Breathe out

Breathe in

Breathe out

Breathe in

Breathe out

Now shift your attention to your head

Look at the chain of thoughts

Some people are always troubled by the chain of thoughts

They want to stop the constant mind chatter

It is a futile activity

The evolutionary process of millions of years has given the boon of having several thoughts at the same time to the human brain.

It is a boon, not a bane.

Simply because the process is not in your control doesn't mean it is defective.

Your attempt should be to understand the process not to criticize it

Train your awareness or focus to observe the formation of random thoughts in mind

Look at the process that leads to such thoughts

Don't try to control them

Don't be judgmental

Don't be critical

Simply look at the way thoughts originate

Understand the process through which the brain develops a thought

It is a knowledge that can only be gained by peering into the mind

Once you understand the process, you'll know that thoughts can't trouble you

Train your awareness regularly

Now, shift your focus to your abdomen

Your gut is one of the most important parts of your body

It holds almost the same amount of neurons as your brain

Scientists even believe that the mind is not only in the brain but also in your gut

Your gut warns you of instinctive feelings

It is your gut feeling that leads to flight or fight response

If you are emotionally disturbed

Your gut gets upset

If you are mentally upset

You have gut troubles

Keep your focus on your gut

We will now do abdominal breathing

It is same as deep breathing

You will simply have to hold the air in your gut

Begin with

Inhalations to the count of 3

1....2....3.

Let the air pass through your lungs and chest to your gut

Hold your breath in the gut to the count of 5

1....2....3....4....5

Exhale slowly through your mouth to the count of 7

1....2.....3.....4....5.....6.....7

Repeat

Inhale to the count of 3

1....2....3.

Let the air pass through your lungs and chest to your gut

Hold your breath in the gut to the count of 5

1....2....3....4....5

Exhale slowly through your mouth to the count of 7

1....2.....3.....4....5.....6.....7

As you breathe from your gut, you'll observe complete calm

The more you focus on your gut

The easier you'll find to train your mind

Repeat once again

Inhale to the count of 3

1....2....3.

Let the air pass through your lungs and chest to your gut

Hold your breath in the gut to the count of 5

1....2....3....4....5

Exhale slowly through your mouth to the count of 7

1....2.....3.....4....5.....6.....7

Relish this calm while you return your breathing to normal

Inhale

Exhale

Inhale

Exhale

Inhale

Exhale

Now Bring your consciousness back to reality

Don't open your eyes yet

Simply try to experience your surrounding with your eyes closed

Feel the sensation air is making on your skin

Feel the warmth or the cold of the surrounding

Move your limbs a bit

Now open your eyes slowly

Remain seated in the same position for a bit longer

Try to feel if there is some tingling sensation in your legs

Feel the peace and calm

Rejoice stresslessness

Feel free to get up at your will.

Conclusion

Thank you for making it through to the end of this book, let's hope it was informative and able to provide you with all of the tools you need to achieve your goals whatever they may be.

This book was a sincere attempt to explain the concept of mindfulness meditation and how you can benefit from it.

The concept of mindfulness meditation has been explained in a practical and doable way. The intent was to make it as much accessible as possible.

Mindfulness meditation is not another fad concept. It is the way of life that can bring great emotional and psychological stability in your life.

The guided meditations are easy to follow and very comprehensive. The intent of these guided meditations is to help you in achieving relaxation and awareness.

This book was aimed at making meditation easily accessible to everyone so that more and more people can benefit from this amazing life science.

You can also get all the benefits of the process by following the simple steps given in the book. I hope that this book is really able to help you in achieving your goals.

Finally, if you found this book useful in any way, a review on Amazon is always appreciated!

CPSIA information can be obtained
at www.ICGtesting.com
Printed in the USA
BVHW042116181020
591193BV00021B/638